A Summary of
Benjamin Graham
and
David Dodd's

Security Analysis

by
Preston Pysh and Stig Brodersen

Security Analysis 100 page summary
copyright © by 100 page summaries.

ISBN: 978-1-939370-17-4

Library of Congress Cataloging-in-Publication Data

Pysh, Preston and Brodersen, Stig
Security Analysis 100 Page Summaries

This publication is designed to provide accurate and authoritative information in regard to the subject matter covered. It is sold with the understanding that neither the authors nor the publisher are registered experts in the subject matter discussed. If legal advice or other expert assistance is required, the services of a competent professional person should be sought.

Table of Contents

on 2ND + readings, just re-read [pencil] markings + writings!

Purpose of Security anal. is to determine whether a stock should be bought/sold or held. It does not deal in qualitative + intuition insights which for me are very imp.

A Note from the Summary Authors

Years ago, I read Security Analysis for the first time. Well, let me rephrase that, I tried to read Security Analysis for the first time. Although I knew the book was full of the most profound investment advice ever written, I obviously struggled with comprehending the information. After talking with countless investors, I found many other people shared the same struggle.

Although Security Analysis might be a difficult book to comprehend, its value is limitless once a firm understanding of the terminology and overarching strategy is gained. That's what we are trying to accomplish with this summary guide. We want this incredible book to be more accessible to the world of investing.

Most importantly, we want to emphasize that this summary guide is not a substitute for the book itself. If anything, our intent is that you read both books, the original and this guide, in a chapter for chapter hand-off. If you read this guide in lock-step with the full length book, you'll find that we have taken the liberty of summarizing very lengthy case studies and important financial findings. This wasn't done to discredit the importance of the subject or the original authors. Instead it's a tool for you to save time and prioritize your focus into areas you deem most important to your investment strategy.

In the end, we truly hope this guide cracks the code of difficulty for Security Analysis. As you go through this summary, you might find topics or terminology that are difficult to understand. If that's the case, we have hours of completely free video content that teaches the basics of common stocks, preferred stocks, and bonds at BuffettsBooks.com. You will also find our user's forum where people can ask questions and get help on any topic. I know it's a location where we like to hangout and discuss potential stock bargains with our valued readers.

Preston and Stig
BuffettsBooks.com

Part I
Survey and Approach

Chapter 1—Summary

The Scope and Limits of Security Analysis.
The Concept of Intrinsic Value.

This chapter lays the core fundamentals of Security Analysis. As you can see, Graham immediately starts the book with the discussion of intrinsic value. Although he doesn't define the details of the concept in this chapter, he indirectly implies that intrinsic value is the result of numerous variables. At the heart of the calculation is the meshing of Book Value and Earnings Power. Graham also discusses his opinion that the stock market is impossible to predict or determine in the short term. He makes a very important claim that the value of your analysis decreases as the element for chance increases. This is a very important idea because it's Graham's scholarly way of saying: *If you're analyzing an unstable business, then you're analysis might be worthless.* He closes the first chapter by clearly describing Security Analysis as a practice of applying facts and identifying unknowns. Applying this practice to stable businesses will help the analyst to ultimately determine the elusive intrinsic value figure and protect their invested capital.

Chapter 1—Outline

Preamble

The term *Analysis* indicates a scientific and methodical study of facts which results in logical conclusions. But investment is not an exact science, and success derives in part from personal skills and chance.

Historically, the field of security analysis developed progressively to 1927, when it was corrupted by a "new era" that was followed by the 1929 market collapse. Analysts were discredited both for creating the crash and for not preventing it.

Three Functions of Analysis:

Given under three headings:

1. Descriptive
2. Selective
3. Critical

1. **Descriptive Function**

   Descriptive analysis requires collecting all the important facts and presenting them in an understandable manner. By doing this, you will:

   - Reveal strong and weak points
   - Make comparisons with similar issues
   - Appraise for future performance.

   Such an analysis is appropriate not only for the investor but also for the speculator.

2. **The Selective Function Of Security Analysis**

   Expresses specific judgment, by determining whether an issue should be bought, held, sold, etc.

   Examples of Analytical Judgments. In this section, Graham provides a couple different examples of bonds and common stocks that traded at bargain prices and expensive prices. The method for determining this comparison was the company's ability to earn and make payments to the investor. He showed that as the market price on the security changed in comparison to the company's ability to earn, so did the intrinsic value of the investment. This analytical comparison would be the framework for Graham's discussions on intrinsic value.

   Intrinsic Value vs. Price. First, we establish the idea that intrinsic value is an elusive idea. We must remember it is only an estimate and not a firm fixed value. Valuation is based on the analyst's opinion of the intrinsic worth of the security:

   - Assets
   - Earnings
   - Dividends
   - Definite prospects

   Prior to the publication of Security Analysis, many believed the value of a business to be directly related to the book value. Graham cautions readers against that perception and argues more variables are obviously part of determining the intrinsic value of a business.

   Intrinsic Value and "Earning Power." In more recent times (about the time when Security Analysis was first published), Graham talks about the new metric for valuation, "earnings power". This idea is that a multiple over the company's earnings is the best way to value a business. This is often referred to as the P/E ratio. Graham also cautions readers that valuing a business solely from the earnings power is also risky and uncharacteristic of a wise analyst.

The Role of Intrinsic Value in the Work of the Analyst. The analyst does not attempt to determine a precise intrinsic value. Instead, he attempts to determine in relative terms whether a common stock or bond purchase provides enough safety to protect the principal invested. Graham then provides historical examples of companies that traded for extremely low prices compared to their earnings and health. He uses these examples to represent the idea that he didn't know the exact intrinsic value, but definitely knew the picks were undervalued.

Flexibility of the Concept of Intrinsic Value. Graham discusses that the range for intrinsic value increases as the uncertainty for a business increases. For example, if a company is expected to have volatile numbers and they aren't predictable, Graham says the intrinsic value could be as broad as $30 to $130 dollars. Although this large range is very difficult to predict, Graham suggests that if the market price falls below this range, the investment may still make practical sense.

More Definite Concept in Special Cases. Graham discusses a scenario where a company had issued two different bonds; One bond for 5% and another for 7%. Due to outside concerns, both bonds were trading on the market for about the same price. From a mathematical standpoint, the 7% bond obviously offers a much better return if both the bonds represent the same safety of repayment. Although this scenario is lucrative to the analyst, it's existence is uncommon.

Principal Obstacles to Success of the Analyst.

- **Inadequate or incorrect data**
- **Uncertainties of the Future:** Graham suggests that predicting an organizations future performance is extremely difficult. He says that past performance is only a rough guideline of what to expect. Senior Securities (i.e. bonds and preferred shares), are somewhat protected against a company's change in future earnings. Whereas common stocks are not. Also, companies that demonstrate stability, often reduce the risk for uncertainties.
- **Irrational Behavior of the Market:** Graham encourages analysts to generally ignore market prices. The only time an analyst should concern himself with the prices is when they are trading uncharacteristically high or low. He briefly mentions the idea that many on Wall Street believe that the stock market prices stocks efficiently. Graham obviously disagrees.

Constantly review "intrinsic value" assessment. Everything changes

Hazard of Tardy Adjustment of Price Value. Since the market price of a particular pick may remain in or out of favor for an extremely long period of time, the analyst may face a hazard with implementing a value approach. By the time the security returns to the original value assessed by the analyst, other factors may have changed the initial estimate. Therefore it is important for the analyst to consistently review the reporting requirements of the company to prevent this from happening.

Relationship of Intrinsic Value to Market Price. The market is akin to a voting machine into which countless people insert their opinion. Those opinions are either based on emotion or reason. The results of those opinions in the short term are unstable and unpredictable. Later, Graham's student, Warren Buffett, would say: *"In the short term the market is a voting machine, but in the long term it tracks value."*

Analysis and Speculation. Any belief that speculation can be made safe in the short term because competent analysis will predict the market price is doomed to failure. This is partly due to the factors described above and largely because of unknown elements which have not been and cannot be included in the analysis.

The Value of Analysis Diminishes as the Element of Chance Increases. Competent analysis provides an advantage but does not guarantee a profit. Analysis is therefore best suited to investment and not to speculation. Analysis may be considered an accessory to speculation but not a *guide*.

3. The Critical Function Of Security Analysis

"Analytical judgments are reached by applying standards to facts." The analyst should seek adequate protective provisions in bonds and preferred stocks. He must be alert to the misrepresentation by accountants. He must be familiar with the policies that management has set in place for the investment. His analysis is directed to the avoidance of mistakes, the correction of abuse, and the protection of the owner in the security.

Chapter 2—Summary

Fundamental Elements in the Problem of Analysis. Quantitative and Qualitative Factors.

Graham starts this chapter with a description of the elements that are fundamental to an analyst's assessment of a security. The descriptions are fairly straight forward. The important highlights are: 1.) The value of a security changes when interest rates change. 2.) The price that an investor pays for a security will impact the return they should expect to receive. 3.) Understand the size and type of business you are analyzing and the stability it possesses.

This chapter then transitions into a discussion of the differences between quantitative and qualitative factors for an analyst. Graham is of the opinion that most factors are qualitative in nature despite having quantitative data. He cautions analysts from forming rock solid opinions about a company's future prospects simply by looking at its quantitative past performance. Again, he stresses the importance of stability and its impact on projecting future results. Graham also states that larger businesses with longer historical results often provided more predictable data for analysts.

Chapter 2—Outline

The purpose of security analysis is to develop a systematic method for determining whether something should be bought, sold, or held. Graham identifies four fundamental elements for doing this.

FOUR FUNDAMENTAL ELEMENTS

- **The Person:** Conclusions from analysis are impersonal; selection of the security rests on factors such as age, wealth, tax status, risk aversion, etc.
- **The Time:** Analytic conclusions will vary with changes in interest rates, performance of the security, and general business outlooks etc.
- **The Price:** Particularly important in considering common stock; fairly important in convertible bonds; of less importance in prime investment bonds. Regardless of the type of security, price is always a consideration.
- **The Security:**
    - *Character of the Enterprise and the Terms of Commitment:* In

So B. Graham would say it has to Be (stock) that offers Better deal than a safe N.S TREASURY Bill/Bond

making a decision about an investment, the smart analyst will not only look at the security and the price. Instead he will also consider the entire enterprise and the terms proposed for ownership. The later often involves an extensive amount of research and work.

♦ *Examples of Commitment on Unattractive Terms:* Although some forms of investment might seem favorable to the analyst, further examination of the terms might uncover risk.

▪ Provisions—Graham discusses the ideas of a preferred share that's junior to a large mortgage (or debt) and of the non-cumulative type (non-cumulative simply means the divided on the preferred stock doesn't have to be paid). This is a security that lacks the safety of a bond and also lacks the rights to dividends or principal payments.

Does company have a lot of debt, Is price reasonable.

▪ Status of the Issue—Does the company you're investing in have the ability to finance more debt if it falls on overruns or difficult times?

▪ Price of the Issue—Do higher priority securities of the same issuer have higher yields? If so, why own a preferred share if it produces a lower yield than the issues ahead of it.

• Note: When businesses are structured, securities follow a prioritization of safety during bankruptcy. This means a bond for company X will have a higher priority than a common stock from company X. This becomes very important during liquidations (or the selling of all the companies assets during bankruptcy) in order to get your invested capital back from the business. If the only value that remains after liquidation can pay for the principal on the bondholders, all other securities would become worthless (i.e. the common stock). In general, the priority of business securities is the following: (safest to riskiest) 1. Loans 2. Bonds 3. Preferred Stock 4. Common Stock

♦ *Examples of a Commitment on attractive Terms:* In this section Graham examines a 5% coupon on a railroad company's bond that was due in 28 years. Its yield to maturity at the time of writing was 9.85%. Below is the same three criteria we used before for unattractive terms.

▪ Provisions—This issue was owned by a company, but their primary contract was with the city of New York to maintain the subways. Therefore the earnings were

Yield To Maturity = is the estimated annual rate of return for a bond if held to maturity date + reinvest the payments at the same rate

The Coupon Rate = the annual income an investor will receive while holding a Bond, can expect to receive

both dependent on the company and the entire city. Therefore the magnitude and stability of the earnings were bigger than one might perceive.

- Status of the Issue—The company had fully capable earnings to meet payments.

- Price of the Issue—It was priced to perform even better the 6% issues by a competing company.

- Graham used this example to highlight a favorable security based on the current circumstances at the time.

Qualitative and Quantitative Factors in Analysis

Graham poses the question; is it better to invest in an attractive enterprise with unattractive terms or better to invest in an unattractive enterprise with favorable terms. Graham sides with the former.

Graham then recommends untrained security analysts to avoid low-grade business on any terms. For the well trained analyst, Graham suggests any security may be attractive depending on the price.

Qualitative and Quantitative Factors in Analysis

Since research on a particular pick could involve unlimited time and effort, Graham suggests the level of detail should be based on the amount of capital invested. For example, $1,000 should require less focus and effort compared to a $500,000 investment.

Technique and Extent of the Analysis Should be Limited by Character and Purposes of the Commitment: The analyst must preserve a sense of comparison; analyze what matters, and ignore what is trivial. For example, if a company owns a patent, should the analyst research the durability of the patent? This can only be determined based on the time available and amount of funds being invested. Each situation is different.

Value of Data Varies with Type of Enterprise: Statistics of a large and long-established corporation are more reliable than those of a new and small enterprise in an industry such as oil where commodity prices fluctuate. Therefore each enterprise needs to be looked at differently but subject to the same principals of value.

Quantitative vs. Qualitative Elements in Analysis: The quantitative element is found in the figures on the balance sheet and income statement. The qualitative element is less defined and in consequence less importance is sometimes attached to it:

- Nature of the business
- Relative position in the industry
- Physical, geographic characteristics
- Management
- Outlook for this corporation, this industry, business in general.

Handwritten margin notes (top right): Nature of Business + mngt. are 2 of the most imp. • is Business ubiquitous a real need by many. does it have a MOAT are owners honest. Founders are best

Handwritten margin notes (left side): So quality features: Is it large/ubiquitous? provides a need to large pop.) good leaders (prefer Founders) is it stable.

Qualitative Factors: Nature of the Business and its Future Prospects: The two most important factors are the nature of the business and its management. Abnormally good or bad conditions may not be everlasting and therefore are hard to predict. This increases risk for the analyst.

The Factor of Management: Tests of management are not scientific, and the best test is in the results over a period of time; there is a tendency to overvalue good management which is already reflected in the price and therefore no additional premium paid on that account.

The Trend of Future Earnings: Drawing conclusions of future performance based on past performance must be used as a rough index and not hard facts. This idea becomes even more important when past performance demonstrates exponential growth or decline. Non-linear past performance is likely unreliable.

Trend Essentially a Qualitative Factor: Graham argues that analysts can't predict future earnings forever; instead all estimates have term limits to reasonable forecasts. Since the analyst is bound by this limit, estimates should be considered qualitative factors.

Qualitative Factors Resist Even Reasonably Accurate Appraisal: In this section Graham makes a strong point that the analyst should not make future earnings *predictions* with the aim of profit—this is speculation. Instead, the analyst should make future earnings *projections* to guard against the risk of paying too much for the security.

Inherent Stability a Major Qualitative Factor: The most important qualitative factor for the analyst is the stability of the investment. Stability means resistance to change and predictability of future results. Graham suggests that stability can be qualitative and quantitative alike. Stability may depend on the nature of the business, i.e. food is always in demand, and luxury goods may not be.

Summary of quantitative and qualitative: The analyst's conclusions must have a numerical basis, follow standards, and survive testing. Stability is of prime importance for the analyst as they make projections for future cash flows from data collected by past results. The numbers may be overturned by knowledge of other, qualitative factors.

Chapter 3—Summary

Sources of Information

As one might suspect, a chapter about stock sources from the 1930's is somewhat outdated. Although more sources of information are available today, the ones Graham mentions in this chapter are still relevant and often preferable. If Graham were alive today, he would most likely caution investors from using financial data from unreliable sources—i.e. many places on the internet. It's important to note that most company's provide their 10Q (quarterly report) and 10K (annual report) in their website's investor relations section. These reports will provide investors with the most accurate financial data because they are required documents by the federal government. This doesn't necessarily mean the documents are 100% truthful, but it does protect the analyst against misrepresented data found on Google, or Morningstar, which is compiled by a computer program.

10Q   10K
important

Chapter 3—Outline

The analyst might seek data on the:

- Terms of the specific issue
- The company
- The industry

For a bond contract an analyst would consult the deed of trust; for a stock issue he would look at the company charter. All of this information is also kept on file with the Securities and Exchange Commission (SEC), and/or from the exchanges directly (NYSE, AE, Nasdaq etc.).

Data on the Company

In this section, Graham provides a background on the reporting requirements of his era. As one might expect, many of optional reporting requirements in the 1930's are now quarterly requirements by the SEC.

Reports to Stockholders (Including Interim News Releases): Reports to stockholders are the prime source of information. Depending on the industry, these may have been issued anywhere from monthly to annually, but quarterly is the usual. The balance sheet will be in the annual report.

The *income account* should show:

- Sales
- Net earnings
- Depreciation and depletion
- interest charges
- Non-operating income in detail
- Income taxes
- Dividends paid
- Surplus adjustments

The *balance sheet* is standardized. Graham criticizes the practice of many companies for only reporting the net figure on their property account. He suggests that depreciation expenses should be shown next to the original purchase price for the assets so the investor could see how much the asset has been depreciated. It's assumed this recommendation was made so the analyst could try and determine the capital expenditures of the business.

Periodic Reports to Public Agencies: Public utilities supply information at regular intervals. This is also required of companies under the jurisdiction of the Interstate Commerce Commission, and even more information is available from the reports of the United States Department of Commerce. There are privately produced specialized reports from sectors of the industry, for instance motor vehicles, oil and gas, and from agencies such as the Dow Jones.

Listing Applications: When a company becomes a publically traded business, listing applications must be filed with the SEC and stock exchange. These applications often provided detailed information about the company's assets and protocol for doing business. These are a great source of information for any investor. Unfortunately, these applications are only filed once.

Registration Statements and Prospectuses: Extensive data for listing with the SEC is required. Critical and relevant data must be included in the underwriters' prospectus for any new issues, but the mere volume of these may deter the average investor.

Miscellaneous Official Reports: Among the many potential sources of information are government commissions into particular industries and the Interstate Commerce Commission. The emphasis for miscellaneous reports should be on the authority that publishes it and whether or not it's official.

Statistical and Financial Publications: Comprehensive manuals are published annually by organizations such as Standard and Poor's and Fitch & Moody's. These types of reports will likely encompass a majority of the analyst's time and effort.

Requests for Direct Information from the Company: The shareholder is an owner of the business, he employs its staff and is entitled to information. If the analyst has questions about the company's performance, he should not hesitate to contact the company's investor relations division to get answers.

Information Regarding the Industry

The United States Department of Commerce publishes on a monthly basis the most comprehensive information. There are numerous almanacs and trade-specific journals an analyst can use to uncover information about entire industries.

[Handwritten note at top: an investment is one upon thorough analyses promises safety of principal & a satisfactory return. If these are NOT met it is SPECULATIVE]

[Handwritten note in left margin: Day traders are speculators]

Chapter 4—Summary

Distinctions between Investment and Speculation

This chapter is a key component of Graham's value investing philosophy: the distinction between investing and speculating. Graham makes the argument that an investor should **protect their principal** while only accepting a **satisfactory return**. This idea is clearly demonstrated by Graham's star pupil, Warren Buffett. Buffett has two quotes that represent this idea:

"Rule 1, don't lose money. Rule 2, don't forget rule 1."

And

"I don't look to jump over 7-foot bars: I look around for 1-foot bars that I can step over."

Although many investors might treat these quotes as clichés, they are deeply rooted fundamentals from this chapter. The first quote addresses the idea of protecting your principal and the second quote represents the idea of accepting a satisfactory return. A firm understanding of this definition is what protects Graham's students during market recessions. Throughout this chapter, Graham mentions the idea that market price has a direct impact on the safety of a security. If analysts can't account for a premium beyond a calculated investment value for the asset, the security is considered a blend of speculation and investment.

Chapter 4—Outline

General Considerations of the Term "Investment"

"Investment is a word of many meanings." It may mean putting money into a business; it might be applied generically to all financial holdings. Regardless of how it's applied, Graham strongly suggests there is a distinct difference between investing and speculation. Failure to distinguish one from the other has led to tragedies such as the collapse of the market in 1929.

> ***Distinctions Commonly Drawn Between the Two Terms:*** Graham suggests that investments are bonds, outright purchases, permanent holdings, and securities that produce income. Speculation on the other hand is often common stocks, purchases on margin, "quick turn" ventures, for profit securities in risky issues. After describing these common interpretations, Graham provides counterarguments for each perception.

Bonds versus Stocks: Although bonds are often viewed as having little risk, this assumption is not always true. In fact, there are low grade bonds with substantial risk and high grade investment stocks with less risk. This section is provided to show that the conclusions that Graham draws in the previous paragraph is not absolute. Instead, it's situational dependent.

Outright vs. Margin Purchase: This idea refers to the method of purchase, not the element of risk. It is implied that owning a stock represents less risk then owning it on margin, but Graham provides a counterargument. He discusses how penny stocks during his era were required to be purchased outright because they displayed too much risk to the lender to allow them to be purchased on margin.

Permanent vs. Temporary Holding: This section refers to the false impression that permanent holdings represent less risk than temporary holdings. Graham dispels this myth by demonstrating that some speculators develop a permanent holding in hopes that they can recuperate their losses over an extended period of time.

Income vs. Profit: It is this comparison that Graham believes is the most difficult to distinguish between speculation and investment. Graham states that before 1928, many investors sought safety of principal with a respectable income. Over time, the mindset shifted from a respectable income to one that focused on increased future income and even an increase in principal. This is where the difference between income and profit separates. Although this is a major factor in determining the difference between speculation and investment, Graham feels the ultimate authority comes from the safety the investment represents.

Standards of Safety: Graham argues that specific standards for measuring safety must be applied by the analyst to avoid speculation. He implies that speculators use psychological means for determining "sound" picks. He discusses the idea that over paying for a security is often the biggest risk to an analyst. Since speculators eventually develop the mindset that no price is too high to pay, investors must avoid this trap by applying tangible standards to the appraisal of each pick.

Proposed Definition of Investment: "An investment operation is one which, upon thorough analysis, promises safety of principal and a satisfactory return. Operations not meeting these requirements are speculative."

All of the individual terms used in his definition have an element of vagueness and are individually open to dispute; collectively, however, the meaning is clear. Graham makes the point that "thorough analysis" involves a profound application of safety and value. To simply purchase a common stock because it's trading 40 times higher than its highest earnings would not represent "thorough analysis."

He clarifies his point further: "An investment operation is one that can be justified on both qualitative and quantitative grounds."

At the end of this section, Graham provides two examples which demonstrate his definition for investment. He provides an example where purchasing a callable preferred stock, on margin, is considered an investment, and the idea of purchasing the same shares before the call date were speculative. The example is provided to off-set preconceived notions that anything is definitive or predictable and that analysts need to possess a firm understanding of all the facts to arrive at an intelligent conclusion. The example truly displays Graham's brilliance for the subject.

Other Aspects of Investment and Speculation

Relation of the Future to Investment and Speculation: Many believe that investment is founded on the past and speculation looks ahead. Graham opposes this idea and states that investment is also reliant on future performance. He then makes the famous quote: *"the future is to be guarded against rather than profited from."* From this quote, he further explains that the speculator is optimistic and dependant on an improving future performance, whereas the investor doesn't rely on an improving future performance to justify selection.

Types of Investment: In this section, Graham simply defines four different types of investment terminology.

- "Business investment: money held in a business"
- "Financial investment: securities"
- "Sheltered investment: securities with small risk due to prior claims on earnings"
- "Analyst's investment: detailed analysis that promises safety of principal and an adequate return"

Types of Speculation: The New York Stock Exchange (NYSE) defines gambling as taking risks without a need (betting on a horse race), whereas speculation is the inherent risk that must be taken by someone.

- "Intelligent speculation is taking a measured risk that seems justified after analysis"
- "Unintelligent speculation is taking a risk without adequate examination of the situation"

Investment and Speculative Components: Graham suggests that it might be useful for the analyst to break down potential purchases into

"The future is to be guarded against rather than profited from" B. Grahman speculative and investment categories. For example, if the market price of a common stock is $35 per share, the analyst may only find $25 of investment value in the pick with $10 of speculative value due to excellent long-term prospects. Therefore any purchase over $25 should be considered partially speculative by the analyst.

Value: Investment, Speculative or Intrinsic: The analyzed value of a company may have both an investment component, but also speculative value, which may properly be considered *intrinsic value* provided it is based on proper analysis. As a result, Graham suggests that the analyst should act as an appraiser of value.

So Speculative may be called INTRINSIC VALUE

Chapter 5—Summary

Classification of Securities

This chapter is a general overview of the different types of securities available to investors. Graham clearly identifies each type according to their associated risk and reward. An important highlight in this chapter is the way analysts should view the prioritization of equity for any organization. If an analyst lacks this important knowledge, they won't understand how each security interacts with superior and subordinate issues of the same organization during financial bankruptcy. The analyst should also be aware that bonds, preferred shares, and common shares may be morphed into hybrid securities. For example, there are convertible bonds which may be converted in common stock. In the end, analysts must be ready to account for the numerous variables associated with any particular pick.

Chapter 5—Outline

The usual classification of securities is bonds and stocks, the latter subdivided into preferred and common stocks. The critical difference between each security is the legal structure of its equity. Bond holders have prior claim on principal and interest which the stockholders do not have. In contrast, the common stockholders own the business and its potential for increased profits. If the business enters bankruptcy, the common stockholder relinquishes ownership of the tangible assets to the bond holder in order to recuperate the principal lent the business.

Objections to the Conventional Grouping

1. *Preferred Stock Grouped with Common:* preferred stocks should be classified with bonds; it is purchased to receive a fixed income with safety of the principal.

2. *Bond Form Identified with Safety:* safety of a bond is totally dependent on the fiscal stability of the company, they have no inherent safety.

3. *Failure of Titles to Describe Issues with Accuracy:* some securities are issued that do not fall conveniently into one or another of these two groups. Although every conceivable variation has been launched, in general they are patterned after bonds, preferred stock, or common stock.

New Classifications Suggested

Graham provides a brief glimpse into his frustration with the naming conventions of his era. He suggests that new classifications are changed to the following categories. This new naming convention is an effort to help inform investors of potential risks and their corresponding rewards. At the top of his list is the safest type of securities that protect an investor's principal and still pays income to the holder.

1. Investment bonds and preferred stocks
2. Speculative bonds and preferred stocks
   a. Convertibles etc.
   b. Low grade senior issues
3. Common stocks

Group "1" includes issues where there is no anticipated change in value, and are held for protection of capital.

Group "2a" the investor looks for safety but also the possibility for profit.

Group "2b" the risk is increased but so is the potential for profit.

Group "3" the intention is profit.

Variations and alternatives modify this simplistic system, such as a bond that would be in Group 1 moves to Group 2a if it is selling at an unduly low price. Furthermore, if a preferred stock holds such a large portion of equity from the common shareholder, the analyst should treat the preferred stock as a substitute for the common equity stake. Frequently the distinction between Groups is one of personal opinion held by the analyst. The important point is not what the purchaser is entitled to demand, but rather what the purchaser will get from owning the security.

Part II
Fixed Value Investments

Chapter 6—Summary

Preferred stock ?
Bonds +

The Selection of Fixed Value Investments

In this chapter, Graham makes a very strong case for finding healthy issuers of fixed income investments (bonds or preferred stock). After briefly discussing the different types of fixed income investments, he quickly transitions into all the risks associated with this form of security. One of the most important highlights of the chapter is his discussion on valuing a fixed income investment from a depression basis opposed to a prosperous one. Graham goes to great lengths to demonstrate to the reader that the safety associated with a fixed income investment is purely related to the issuer's ability to meet payments with coupons or dividends and little else. His final guidance is straight forward: When dealing with fixed income investments, avoid trouble from the start because recuperating the principal after bankruptcy is extremely difficult and unlikely.

Chapter 6—Outline

The fixed value grouping comprises:

1. "High grade straight bonds and preferred stocks."
2. "High grade privileged issues with remote privilege of no consequence."
3. "Common stocks with guarantee or privilege rendering them high grade senior issues."

Basic Attitude toward High-grade Preferred Stocks: Graham's opinion is that preferred stock of the highest quality should be valued the same way as high-grade bonds. Although preferred stock is inferior to bonds, it shouldn't matter if the company has ample financial capacity to make payment. Finding preferred stock of this quality is extremely rare and isn't considered normal.

Preferred Stocks not Generally Equivalent to Bonds in Investment Merit: Usually, the average preferred stock should be ranked lower than the high-grade bond. The reason for this position is that preferred stock does not have protection for a dividend payment "beyond reasonable doubt." In fact, if the preferred stock is non-cumulative, the business has no obligation to make dividend payments even when called.

Is Bond Investment Logical?: In this section, Graham describes the market crash (from 1929) and considers it an anomaly that would not be repeated.

He counters that idea with the caution that "complete security" for bonds does not exist.

Bond Form Inherently Unattractive: Quantitative Assurance of Safety Essentials: Analysts are cautioned against the mindset that bonds guarantee security. If the analyst is surrendering their claim on the company's profits, they should be rewarded by a reasonable level of safety for assuming such a limitation.

Major Emphasis on the Avoidance of Loss: Bond selection is a *negative art* that follows the axiom: "if there is difficulty or doubt, the security should be declined."

Four principles for the Selection of Issues of the Fixed-Value Type:

I think possible depression

- Safety is measured by the ability of the issuer to meet obligations—not by contractual rights
- The ability to meet obligations should be assessed in terms of depression, not prosperity
- Lack of safety is not compensated by a high dividend or coupon
- Selection of bonds should follow rules of exclusion and quantitative tests (like banks perform when issuing loans)

I. Safety Not Measured by Lien but by Ability to Pay

This section can be summarized by a basic question: If a friend owed you money, but was broke, how would they repay you?—Graham suggests they wouldn't.

In theory, if a business fails, the bond holder recovers his money from assets; but that often fails because:

- Property values shrink when the business fails.
- There is difficulty in establishing legal rights.
- There are inherent delays in receivership.

So stay w/ Gov Bonds is my rational

Lien is No Guarantee against Shrinkage of Values: The assessed value of the property is often related to its use; when it is not used, the value declines. What value is a specialized factory if it produces TV antennas which have no market?

Impracticable to Enforce Basic Legal Rights of Lien Holder: Although bondholders might in theory be entitled to sell the property of a failed business, in reality the courts rarely allow the transaction; usually they are given securities in a reorganized corporation. Only on rare occasions are bond holders paid in full during a corporate default. If one is lucky enough to experience such a payment, it's always the result of a long and tiresome delay.

Delays are Wearisome: Going into receivership causes a loss of value of all property and holdings. The more value and assets involved, the longer the receivership takes and the more the value is depreciated.

Note: Receivership is a bankruptcy situation in which a receiver is appointed by courts or creditors to run the company. The receiver may be appointed as a matter of private proceedings or by a governing body. The ultimate decision is how the remaining assets will be managed and distributed. This is typically done in a company liquidation situation.

Basic Principle is to Avoid Trouble: To avoid trouble is better than seeking protection after it occurs. From this principle, three simple explanations are provided:

1. "The absence of a lien* is of minor consequence"; unsecured debentures* of a strong company might be just as safe.

2. To buy the "highest yielding obligation of a sound company" is in itself unsound because if the junior issues are not safe, neither are the senior issues.

3. "Senior liens are to be favored, unless junior obligations offer a substantial advantage." This idea is valid only if the protection of the total debt is adequate and the monetary advantage is substantial.

Special Status of Underlying Bonds: In this section, Graham describes a practice during his era where underlying bonds out prioritized "first issue" bonds. He provides examples of underlying bonds throughout the text and then concludes the section by saying ordinary investor should disregard these issues in their calculations.

*Note:

- A lien is a legal claim of one person/business upon the property of another person/business to secure the payment of a debt.

- A debenture is an unsecured loan certificate issued by a company or government that is backed by general credit rather than by specified assets. Debentures have no collateral. Purchasing a treasury bond is considered a debenture because the issue is not backed by any tangible asset or security.

only faith in USA

So Treasury Bond is a debenTure

Debenture — has no backing.

Chapter 7—Summary

The Selection of Fixed Value Investments: Second and Third Principles

The primary objective of this chapter is to identify further considerations for the selection of fixed income securities. During the first section of this chapter, Graham reiterates the idea that bonds should be analyzed from a depression basis. He warns the analyst that no sector is depression proof, but analysis of past performance during previous recessions will provide clues into a security's success during such events. An important highlight from this section is the idea that "good" debt is when the company is using financed capital for an opportunity or expansion that might require a quick entry to market. This type of debt can be handled by the company's future earnings and repaid from operating activities. "Bad" debt is when the business is required to borrow in order to sustain operations. This determination is much easier for modern investors due to the advent of the cash flow statement. If analysts are considering the financial health of the fixed income issuer, they would be strongly advised to assess the debt from the cash flow statement.

In the last section, Graham strongly encourages analysts to not compromise their assumed risk for an increased reward. If risk is assumed, it should be in the form of paying a cheaper price (therefore lowering the principal required to acquire the security), instead of accepting a higher coupon or dividend. This is a very important concept for value investors because it once again minimizes the loss of principal.

Chapter 7—Outline

II. Bonds Should be Bought an a Depression Basis

A sound investment must be able to withstand adversity, and enterprises that have withstood adversity may be favored by investors.

> **Presumption of Safety Based upon Either the Character of the Industry or the Amount of Protection:** Investment in a depression proof enterprise such as a utility may be safer than a major corporation that's not protected by demand or consumption during a depression.

> **No Industry Entirely Depression-proof:** There is no such thing as "depression proof." The investor should look for industries least likely to be affected by a depression—it's all relative.

Investment Practice Recognizes Importance of Character of the Industry: Historically some industries and public utilities have been more stable than others, and equally their degree of stability has altered with time. This changing dynamic is something the analyst must consider when assessing an organization's ability to continue meeting future payments on fixed income securities.

Depression Performance as a Test of Merit: In this section, Graham displays a graphical chart comparing the performance of railroads to public utilities. The importance of the chart is to demonstrate how both sectors performed during a depression basis. He recommends that this approach is applied to securities that analysts would like to assess in the future.

Various Causes of Bond Collapses:

1. "Excessive funded debt of utilities": defaults were caused by over-extended debt, not by lack of earnings.
2. "Stability of railroad earnings overrated": this resulted from diminished earnings and a failure to recognize changes in transportation methods.
3. "Depression performance of industrial bonds": there was a sudden disappearance of earnings which was best tolerated by the largest companies that were performing well before the Depression struck.

Unavailability of Sound Bonds No Excuse for Buying Poor Ones: No excuse can be made for the purchase of unsound securities. The investor should never be tempted by the lack of a good opportunity to venture into a poor one.

Conflicting Views on Bond Financing: There are two incorrect theories: a) that issuing a bond is a statement of financial weakness and b) that bonds are only issued when companies cannot issue stock.

Proper Theory of Bond Financing: A reasonable amount of funded debt is an advantage (typically rooted in the company's ability to take their product or service to market quickly), provided it can be handled under all conditions. If the company is obligated to acquire debt (meaning they need to issue debt to simply pay their bills and expenses), this is a statement and signal that the bond is unsafe. This situation is not only bad for the company, but also the bond holder.

Unsound Policies Followed in Practice: In this section, Graham describes a situation in 1927-1929 where companies were frantically trying to pay off debt. Companies took the practice so far that they started issuing new shares to raise capital, which in turn paid for the debt obligations. Graham highlights the importance for shareholders to consider the objective of such actions. Is the objective for management to simplify their problems or is the objective to pay off high interest debt? If the objective is the later, shareholders may benefit from such an action. If the objective is paying off low interest debt, shareholders are losing value at the expense of poor management.

Significance of the Foregoing to the Investor: Graham suggests that whenever there is money available to invest, it is invested. The problem lies in the leaders inability to manage investments when higher yielding securities disappear from the market place. During these situations, analysts need to accept a lower yielding security to ensure the protection of principal instead of choosing more yield in a second rate issue.

Summary: Bonds should be bought on their ability to withstand a depression or recession; relative safety is found in companies of: a) dominant size, and b) substantial margin of earnings over bond interest.

III. Third Principle: Unsound To Sacrifice Safety for Yield

Traditionally a numerical rating is applied to interest rates as compared to risk. This is similar to the actuarial methods of the insurance industry to investments. Graham discusses the proposed relationship between reward and the statistical chance of failure, but declares the idea impractical in reality.

No mathematical Relationship between Yield and Risk: Prices and yields often depend on popularity. Graham suggests that the public's familiarity with the issuing company and its ability to be quickly sold on the market is a considerable factor in the market price of bonds.

Self-Insurance Generally Not Possible in Investment: The investor is interested in avoiding risk, not to be paid for assuming it. In this section Graham provides a great example of an investor that purchases a low yielding bond for $1,000 that pays an annual coupon of $20. He then describes a second bond that sells for the same price, but pays a $70 coupon but runs a 1 in 20 risk of complete failure. He suggests this situation is similar to the same risk insurance companies assume when offering full coverage for a house fire. The difference is the insurance companies are prepared to assess the statistical likelihood of such a situation, where the analyst must account for more variables. Graham argues that the additional $50 isn't worth the loss of principal for owning a security that has 1 in 20 odds of failure. The 1 in 20 odds where determined from a previous discussion at the start of this section; it's located in the complete book after the title for the *Third Principle: Unsound to Sacrifice Safety for Yield*.

The Factor of Cyclical Risks: An insurance company spreads risk over a large field; the investor has only a small field and cannot afford a program entailing a small sample size with large risk.

Risk and Yield are Incommensurable: Comparing risk to yield is not definitive. Analysts can only make reasonable assumptions on how a particular security may perform and then compare it to the level of reward they're willing to assume. Graham mentions, yet again, that the analyst should not pay a par value for a risky bond that has a high yield. Instead, he should pay a considerable discount below the par value, therefore minimizing his risk of principal.

Fallacy of the "Businessman's Investment": During Graham's era there was an impression that foreign bonds and/or risky bonds were considered the "Businessman's Investment". He pokes fun at the idea and claims it's illogical.

Reversal of Customary Procedure Recommended: Don't start with inspecting the safest fixed income issues on a list and work down. Instead, start with the security that represents a minimal threshold of safety and work up on the list. This way the analyst protects themselves from going deeper into the list—likely resulting in the purchase of an unsafe issue.

Chapter 8—Summary

Specific Standards for Bond Investment

This chapter initiates the discussion of standards an analyst should apply to the purchase of bonds. The dialogue initiated in this chapter extends over the next three chapters as well. Graham forms his foundation for analysis by starting with the criteria that the New York Savings Bank (NYSB) uses for purchasing fixed income bonds. We find that the NYSB applies seven criteria to their risk management procedures. Graham uses these criteria as a baseline since the NYSB is obligated by law to protect the principal of their clients. After laying out his methodology for analysis, Graham discusses each of the seven criteria in detail. This chapter covers the first two criteria the NYSB uses.

1. Nature and Location—Graham believes an analyst should have a broader pool of choices for the bonds they can select compared to the NYSB. He doesn't specifically name which types of enterprises he would add to the NYSB list. It appears Graham agrees with the Bank's decision to limit the selection of Bonds to the United States—with the exception of Canada.

2. Size—Graham discusses the specific benchmarks associated with the bank's basis for determining secure bonds. He argues that more emphasis should be placed on the issuer's ability to repay the obligations than the sheer size of a municipal government or business.

Chapter 8—Outline

IV. Fourth Principle: Definite Standards of Safety must be applied

The selection of high-grade bonds is a process of elimination. As a result, the process works quite well when applied to specific standards and rules. Graham states that individual investors are generally exposed to the same risks as large institutions that invest in similar securities. As a result, he recommends the implementation of similar rules and regulations that savings banks use for fixed income investments. Since they are required and obligated by law to minimize their exposure to risk, Graham recommends their model of risk management as a baseline for his analysis.

New York Savings Bank Law as a Point of Departure: In this section, Graham recommends the New York Savings Bank as a reputable source for applying a template of risk mitigation. Although this bank is better than many, Graham cautions the analyst that government legislation was drawn up in many different ways to impose regulations that did not necessarily have the welfare of the investor at heart. As a result, these rules should be regarded loosely and amended if new metrics prove more useful and secure.

General Criteria Prescribed by the New York Statute: According to the statute, bond investments should be analyzed by the following criteria:

1. *Nature* and *location* of the business
2. *Size* of the business
3. *Terms* of Issue
4. *Record* of solvency and dividend payment
5. Relation of *earnings* to interest requirements
6. Relation of *value* of the property to funded debt
7. Relation of *stock* capitalization to funded debt.

These seven criteria will be discussed in great detail over the next three chapters. Graham will highlight areas where he agrees with the New York Savings Bank and also offer recommendations for improvement.

1. Nature and Location

Graham describes the New York regulations for allowing the purchase of some bonds and the exclusion of others as "Striking". At the time of Graham's writing, this was the bank's protocol:

- "Admitted: US government and municipal bonds; bonds issued by railroads and certain utilities; bonds secured by 1st mortgage in real estate."
- "Excluded: Bonds of foreign governments and corporations; bonds of street railways and water companies; public utility debentures; all industrial bonds; financial companies bonds."

The Fallacy of Blanket Prohibitions: Graham considered the "acceptable" list as too sweeping against industry and too narrow, and that the narrowness of choice caused a limiting factor in the size of the market, driving investors to less worthy choices in the categories that were considered "acceptable".

Individual Strength May Compensate for Inherent Weakness of a Class: Securities of individual companies should be examined rather than blanket acceptance of one class to the exclusion of others.

The 1938 Amendment to the Banking Law: In 1938, NY legislature changed their position on blanket provisions—due to the complaints that Graham and others raised. The new law was quite odd. A bank's restrictions on certain bonds were to be amended on an individual basis if 20 savings banks requested it. In Graham's view this worked well in practice, but questions the logic of setting up a list of forbidden securities only to have it amended on demand.

Obligations of Foreign Governments: Although Graham opposed blanket exclusions, he agreed with the decision to disallow the purchase of foreign bonds. His argument was fourfold.

The factor of political expediency: If payment is withheld, foreign government debt is not enforceable, and non-payment has become familiar.

The foreign trade argument: Although foreign investment is needed to increase the export trade of American businesses, the investor should not make his personal financial decisions on idealistic reasoning.

The individual record argument: It is suggested some countries are more creditworthy than others, and some have been accepted as such by the laws of particular States. At the conclusion of this section, Graham argues that only Canada, Holland, and Switzerland demonstrated "unquestionable investment ratings" during his era.

Two-fold objection to purchase foreign government bonds: Generally speaking, foreign bonds should be avoided for two reasons. 1) the basis for obtaining credit is fragile. 2) the past performance is unsatisfactory. Graham then provides Canada as the sole exception to his doubts.

Bonds of Foreign Corporations: In theory no company should do better than the country in which it is located because the government could simply declare state ownership. Although this is a possibility, experience has shown large and reliable foreign corporations, with bonds issued in US dollar denominations, proved reliable although their own country was not. Nevertheless, foreign corporations are not, in general terms, any more attractive than foreign governments.

2. Size

Small companies and small municipalities are vulnerable and their bonds should not be considered suitable for the conservative investor. No mathematical definition of when an issuing body was too "small" is given.

Provisions of New York Statute: Throughout this section, Graham provides the specifics that the NYSB employed for determining the acceptable size of issuers in the 1930's. For example, municipal bonds required a population of 10,000 in adjacent states and 30,000 elsewhere; railroads had to have 500 miles of track and annual operating revenues of ten million nominal dollars, etc.

Criticisms of requirements: Although Graham agrees that the issuer should be of reasonable size, he disagrees with many of the metrics used by the NYSB. He suggests that the underlying theory of cash flow and ability to repay the holder of the security is more meaningful.

Industrial Bonds and Factor of Size: Although the NYSB is not able to invest in industrial bonds, Graham disagrees with this decision and feels these bonds are safe if tested against strict standards. He recommends limiting selections to the six largest corporations in any particular industry.

Large Size Alone No Guarantee of Safety: Biggest is not universally best, and in particular should not be applied to municipalities and utilities, but only to industries.

Other Provisions Rejected: In this section, Graham rejects the idea that a ten million dollar earnings requirement is imposed on the NYSB to purchase railroad bonds. He assumes the provision is required so high volume securities will be acquired and therefore be more marketable when sold. This way the bank could quickly sell the bonds if they desired. Graham believes too much emphasis is place on securing marketable bonds and therefore disagrees with the requirement.

Chapter 9—Summary

Specific Standards for Bond Investment (Continued)

As mentioned in Chapter 8, Graham continues his assessment of the seven criteria the New York Savings Bank (NYSB) employs for finding sound bond investments. Below is a brief summary of the three criteria discussed in this chapter:

3. Terms of issue—In general, Graham finds the methods of the NYSB outdated with respect to its treatment of mortgage and debenture investments. Graham illustrates that income bonds (different than regular bonds: refer to Chapter 16 for more information) and preferred stock should be analyzed similarly. He concludes this section by cautioning analysts against the myth that short term bonds are more secure than long term bonds. Although the NYSB disagrees, Graham provides convincing arguments for his opinion.

4. Record of solvency and dividend payments—Graham starts this chapter by describing the importance of finding bond issuers that have a long standing history of completing payment obligations. When assessing the strength of a business's bonds, the NYSB uses the company's dividend history as the primary means for determining an ability to make payment. Although Graham acknowledges that this might represent financial strength, he cautions against this practice and encourages analysts to draw conclusions from the income statement and balance sheet. He even makes the valid argument that if a company is paying a dividend, it's releasing capital to the owners without the ability to recall or use the money during difficult times. This, therefore, may inhibit the company's ability to meet future obligations on the bond.

5. Relation of earnings to interest requirements—Graham describes his opinion that the <u>coverage ratio (or ratio of earnings to fixed coupon obligations) is the most significant factor in determining the safety of a bond</u>. He provides three methods for determining the coverage ratio and recommends—the "overall method". This method adds up all the fixed obligations, regardless of the issues priority, and compares it to the company's net income (or profit after tax). Although the NYSB has rigid coverage requirements, Graham recommends that the standards be loosened. He also

prescribes more flexibility for companies that don't meet the NYSB requirements with three considerations: (a) a rising trend of profits; (b) a good current showing; and (c) a satisfactory coverage ratio in all years studied. Finally, Graham discusses an extremely important concept with respect to interest rates and the market price of bonds. He cautions investors from buying long term bonds when interest rates are low due to the likelihood of losing the principal on their investment if sold on a secondary market.

Chapter 9—Outline

3. The Terms of the Issue (Titled in the book: The Provisions of the Issue)

Safety and Security is of prime importance. The laws by the State of New York accept public utility bonds only when secured by mortgages. An exception is made for unsecured railroad and income bonds if earnings and dividend records meet severe stipulated rules.

- Note: An income bond is one in which the issuer isn't obligated to pay any coupons, but must repay the par value at a specified term. The provisions of income bonds vary greatly among the different issues, the basic distinction being between those on which interest must be paid if earned and those over which the directors have a greater or lesser measure of discretion. Generally speaking, income bonds are more similar to preferred stocks than ordinary fixed obligations. Refer to Chapter 16 for more information.

Obsolete and Illogical Restrictions: Graham argues that excluding certain issues doesn't make practical sense. He's open to the idea of investing in various types of fixed income securities; from first issues to debentures. He emphasizes the importance of understanding whether a specific issue has limitations on future issues being prioritized higher. In the end, the company's ability to meet its obligations is the top consideration.

Income Bonds in Weaker Position than Debentures: In this section, Graham debunks the idea that Debentures are less secure than income bonds. To prove his point, Graham explains that debentures are required to make payments (despite not being backed by tangible assets); where as income bonds are not required to make coupon payments. Instead income bonds are like preferred stock and management has the discretion to pay the holder when they feel necessary. As a result, Graham believes the mandatory coupon payment for a debenture provides less risk to the holder than an income bond.

Standards of Safety Should Not Be Relaxed Because of Early Maturity:
If a bond has a short-term maturity of three years the investor might
relax their standards and view a larger margin of safety. Graham cautions
analysts of this misperception. He argues that companies in financial
difficulties may launch short-term bonds only because their credit rating
could not justify a long-term issue.

Distinctions between Short and Long Maturities of the Same Issue.
Graham makes the argument that if two different bonds, a short term and
a long term, are issued and secured by the same company, the risk is no
different for either bond if the short-term issue can't be paid at maturity.
After explaining this idea, he provides multiple examples to demonstrate
his conclusion.

4. Record of Interest and Dividend Payments

The investor should ensure the issuer of the bond has a long record of financial
stability and should avoid those which do not have a history of success.

Provisions of New York Statute. Using this idea, the statute for the State
of New York requires a 10 year history of payments on issues from other
states, and a 25 year history from municipalities, 6 years for railroads and
8 years from other public utilities. Graham then discusses the difficulty
in analyzing a municipality's stability and aptitude to make future
payments. This is especially true when considering the lack of control
one has over the municipality's decision to issue more debt if new leaders
are elected. In this idea, Graham revisits the comment that an investor
should not take a higher return for risk, instead they should pay a lower
principal. Therefore, when a municipal government issues new bonds at
higher interest rates, because of the risk of default, the investor should be
skeptical of such investments.

A Dilemma and a Suggested Solution. Although many variables impact
the analyst's ability to determine the financial health of a municipality,
Graham suggests that strict quantitative tests could be developed. The
tests would focus on the population size, the revenues received, and
the current liabilities. In the end, if the analyst determines the local
government can repay the obligation, then the higher return isn't a
function of assuming more risk. Instead it's a higher yield for his time
and effort to conduct the research to find such a security.

The Dividend Record. Many statutes for states in the 1930's required
banks to only purchase corporate bonds from companies that had a clean
5 year record of paying dividends.

Dividend Record Not Conclusive Evidence of Financial Strength. Although

Graham agrees that dividend paying companies often demonstrated stronger performance, he argues that non-dividend paying companies should not be eliminated from consideration because of this blanket requirement. The alternative argument is the payment of a dividend financially weakens the corporation (because the released capital can't be returned to the company accounts), which may not be in the interests of the bond-holder.

The Role of the Dividend Record in Bond Investment. Make no mistake, the balance sheet and income statement provide better clues about a company's ability to meet future coupon payments than historical divided performance. One advantage of owning bonds from a company that pays dividends to its common shareholders is that the dividend can be used as a warning signal to the analyst. If the dividend is withheld or reduced to the common shareholders, the health of the bond may be in jeopardy.

5. Relation of Earnings to Interest Requirements

Although many analysts judge the safety of a bond by comparing the company's earnings to its interest obligations, the New York statute places emphasis elsewhere. Instead, it approaches a bonds security from the company's ability to pay a dividend. Graham has serious objections to this position. He argues that determining the health of a corporate bond is fairly straight forward considering interest charges are fixed. Therefore, it's very obvious to the analyst what expenses need to be covered.

Requirements of the New York Law. In this section, Graham specifically identifies the few requirements that were actually identified by the NYSB for earnings coverage.

Companies that specialize in railroad mortgages and equipment obligations must earn 1.5 times the fixed charges in 5 of the 6 previous years.

Other railroad issues must have earned 2 times the fixed charges in 5 of the 6 previous years.

For public utilities, the previous 5 years earnings must be 2 times the total interest charges.

Three Phases of the Earnings Coverage: attention is given to the way in which earnings are calculated, how much needs to be coverage over fixed fees, and the time to validate the test.

1. Method of Computation.

The Prior-deductions Method. This method was commonly used before 1933, but was found to be misleading and invalid after the Great

Depression. The method subtracts fixed interest from the earnings for each preceding bond. The coverage ratio is determined after each subtraction. For example:

Average Earnings	$1,500,000
Deducting Interest on first 6s	$500,000 earned 3 times
Balance	$1,000,000
Interest on debenture 7s	$300,000 earned 3.3 times

As one can see, it appears the debenture 7s have more coverage than the first issue. This method is obviously misleading.

The Cumulative-deductions Method. Under this method, interest on junior and senior bonds are combined and compared to the company's earnings. For example, if a company's earnings were $1,000,000, and the interest on the first issue was $200,000, and the interest on the second issue was $300,000, the following coverage ratios would exist:

The first issue would have a coverage ratio of 5.0— ($1,000,000/$200,000)

The second issue would have a coverage ratio 2.0— ($1,000,000/$500,000)

The ratio of earnings divided by the combined interest payments is the essence of this method. Many investors would regard this as a sound procedure for assessing the risk of a security.

The Total-deductions or "Over-all" Method. Although this method is similar to the cumulative deductions method, it offers a more conservative approach. Since Graham suggests that all bonds (regardless of priority) are dependent upon each other, he expects all issues to fail if the payment of one cannot be completed. Using the same example as above, the coverage ratio would be 2.0 for both the first and second issue. This is the method that the NYSB uses and it's also the method Graham endorses.

2. Minimum Requirements for Earnings Coverage. In this section, Graham suggests that the coverage ratios that the NYSB used are longer relevant. He suggested that the following coverage ratios where used in the 1930's: 1.75 for public utilities, 2 for railroads, and 3 for industrials.

3. The Period Comprised by the Earnings Test. Although the NYSB assesses the five previous years for determining the safety of an issue, Graham suggests that the most recent years are the most important. An analyst that adopts the methods of the NYSB may invest in companies that have demonstrated a strong average performance, but currently demonstrates insufficient earnings to support safety of future payments. This is undesirable and should be avoided. Graham recommends adjusting the average window of performance to suit a representative timeframe of typical business performance.

Other Phases of the Earnings Record. The analyst is encouraged to pay attention to other factors like the current trend, the minimum figure, and the current figure. These considerations are important but don't necessarily allow the analyst to employ fixed rules against their selection. As discussed in earlier chapters, an understanding of these qualitative features is important.

Unfavorable Factors May Be Offset. As an analyst considers (a) a rising trend of profits (b) a good current showing, and (c) an acceptable margin over interest charges in all the years studied, they might find a bond that doesn't meet every criterion. In this case, the analyst should not immediately dismiss the security. Instead, they should potentially raise the average coverage ratio viewed over a certain number of years to see if average trends represent a more holistic view of the company. If poor current conditions overshadow such an assessment, this approach is not recommended. In the end, the analyst must make sound judgments of their own to determine which course of action is most secure.

The Relation of the Coupon Rate to the Earnings Coverage. In this section, Graham raises a thoughtful question: Can a bond be safe simply because it has a low interest rate? For example, if company 1 has a 2% bond issued, and company 2 has a 4% bond issued, the coverage ratio for company 1 will be twice the coverage of company 2 (assuming the earnings are exactly the same for both businesses).

1. Effect of Coupon Rate on Safety. Graham's main point in this section is that good companies fetch a lower interest rate compared to risky companies. This means that good credit produces better credit.

2. Effect of a Rise in Interest Rates on Safety. A major consideration for the bond investor is the idea that rising interest rates negatively affect the market value of bond. From the company's point of view, coverage ratios will remain intact during rises in interest rates as long as the bond doesn't mature. If the bond matures during rises in interest rates, the company may be forced to issue new bonds at higher rates. "The practical conclusion must be that if the investor considers a rise in interest rates probable, he should not buy long-term, low-coupon bonds, no matter how strong the company." Instead the investor should consider short-term issues. Inversely, if an investor considers a drop in interest rates probable, he should buy long-term bonds that meet significant levels of safety.

3. Relative Attractiveness of the Two Bonds. Graham discusses the idea that a 5.5% bond may be less attractive than a 3% bond because the company may fall into difficult times due to less cash flow from paying high obligation. This would likely result in a reduced market price for the 5.5% bond. Graham then caveats his entire position by claiming the 3% bond also represents risk because it will be discounted more severely if interest rates rise. This section is a great example of Graham's relentless methods for identifying risk and the countless variables one must consider before choosing a safe security. He leaves the reader questioning which approach is more preferable, but prescribes no definitive solution. In short, he leaves the reader thinking about the complexities they face.

Chapter 10—Summary

Specific Standards for Bond Investment (Continued)

This chapter is a continuation of the two previous chapters and it addresses the sixth criteria the New York Savings Bank (NYSB) uses for securing safe bonds. Below is a summary of the sixth criteria:

6. Relation of value of the property to funded debt—Graham makes no hesitations in discounting the value of tangible assets that secure a bond investment. He insists that earnings power is a true display of safety opposed to the tangible asset that back the bond. He argues that as the earnings power diminishes, so does the value of the tangible asset that produces the earnings. Graham also describes the idea that many of the assets are specialized and may be cheaper to reproduce than sell on a secondary market. He describes the practice of many appraisers misrepresenting assets in an effort to mislead management or investors. Graham is of the opinion that many tangible assets will not fetch the asking price the company lists on the balance sheet due to numerous different factors. As a result, the type of property and its usefulness/demand to society is a major factor in determining the safety that property provides for the bond-holder.

Chapter 10—Outline

The Relation of the Value of the Property to the Funded Debt

The soundness of the bond rests on the ability of the issuing corporation to support its financial obligations, and much less on the potential value of its property for a lien. With that in mind, there is no purpose in devising a minimal pledged level of property value to support the bond, although that is not the view of the State authorities who may require, for instance, property to the value of two thirds in excess of the bond issue.

Special Types of Obligations.

1. **Equipment Obligations:** Equipment that can be put up for sale and used elsewhere, such as a car, has a market value and is therefore a better safeguard than a lien on non-removable property. *Equipment trust certificates* may be issued against specific items of use by the corporation, for instance, again, a car. Although these certificates promise safety at

time of sale, the debtor may only receive 50% of what he expects. In the end, the bond-holder needs to be skeptical of the value of tangible property that backs the safety of the security.

2. Collateral-Trust Bonds: In this section, Graham describes how a collateral-trust bond works. In short, these are bonds that are secured by common stock or other bonds, often of the same corporation. Graham makes no hesitation in identifying that these types of bonds are reliant on each other's success. If one issue fails, all the bonds might fail—like a chain that has a weak link. These bonds offer very little security if issued from the same corporation or subsidiary. The real security for issues of this kind will lie in a profound understanding of the indenture, which dictates the priority, and preference of actions during default.

3. Real Estate Bonds: The value of the property is often directly related to the success of the corporation. As a result, a failing business's assets potentially lose value when the earnings of the business decline. Graham provides a great example how a single family home could be viewed as a safe loan because of the rental value the property could obtain. For example, if a home cost $10,000 and it could receive $1,200 a year in rent, the owner could easily meet fixed loan payments on the debt. Graham then provides a counter example for an industrial property that was purchased for an expensive price but produces very little income compared to the fixed debt obligations. The example is Graham's caution to analysts from assuming corporate property is worth its appraised value.

Property Values and Earning Power Closely Related: Continuing from the previous section Graham suggests that the value of property is directly related to the earnings it can produce. He forcefully cautions investors that this is not true for buildings that were erected for special purposes and manufacturing.

Misleading Character of Appraisals: In this section, Graham discusses his frustration with the appraisal profession during the 1920's. He proclaims that appraisers were simply misleading investors with appraisals that were 2/3rds higher than actual values.

Abnormal Rental Used as Basis of Valuation: Further continuing his complaints of financial appraisals in the 1920's, Graham discusses the oversupply of rental buildings that occurred at the end of the decade.

Debt Based on Excessive Construction Costs: Over-valuation led to over-building which raised construction costs. When the market caught up, the loan against the expensive costs could not be supported.

Weakness of Specialized Buildings: A loan against a house will generally find another person willing to assume the property if necessary;

this may not be true of a hospital or factory.

Values Based on Initial Rentals Misleading: Rentals obtained on a new building are higher than can be obtained for an old building. The duration of the bond issue needs to account for a declining premium for rent due to the age of the building.

Lack of Financial Information: Real estate financing is characterised by private holdings and failure to disclose financial details required from public companies. Nasty surprises like unpaid taxes can often be revealed only too late.

Suggested Rules of Procedure: For single family dwellings, the lender should be sure the amount lent is not more than two thirds the value of the property as determined by the market assessment. If market prices are uncharacteristically high, the appraisal should discount the potential overvaluation. The usual real estate bond is a participation in a first mortgage for a corporation. In this case, the lender should fully understand the costs associated with constructing the property and not exceed the mortgage by 50%. Additionally, there should be a conservatively structured income account that accounts for vacancies and a building that doesn't fetch the premium of a newly constructed property. This account should demonstrate quality coverage over the net income. Additional considerations are the character of the neighborhood and the potential changes that could occur over time.

Chapter 11—Summary

Specific Standards for Bond Investment (Concluded)

This chapter discusses the last category that the New York Savings Bank (NYSB) uses to find sound bond investments. Up until this point in the analysis, Graham has focused on the issuing company's ability to meet annual coupon payments. To do this he has compared the company's earnings (from the income statement) to fixed debt obligation (also on the income statement). Now, he covers the final piece of the puzzle and ensures that the company has the proper resources to cover the principal payment (or par value) once the bond matures. In order to account for this important aspect of the bond's final performance characteristics, Graham compares the principal on the bond (from the balance sheet) to the common shareholder's equity (also on the balance sheet). Additionally, Graham compares the bond's total principal to the current market price of the company's common shares. He provides numerous examples throughout this chapter to demonstrate why this type of comparison is conducive to finding a safe and reliable bond. At the conclusion, Graham summarizes the quantitative requirements from all four chapters for the selection of a sound bond investment.

Chapter 11—Outline

Relation of Stock Capitalization to Bonded Debt

The amount of stock that follows all the different bonds issued by a company (senior and junior issues combined), is always going to be the resources that remain after all debts are fulfilled. In other words, the common shareholder's equity is the figure that Graham is now going to compare to the par value of the whole bond issue.

Standards Prescribed by the New York Law. For the bonds of public utilities the statute enforced by the State of New York requires:

    (1) All combined mortgage debt will be less than 60% of the assessed property value:

    (2) Capital stock (or the common stock and preferred stock combined) at book value will not be less than two thirds of mortgaged debt.

You'll notice that this two-prong requirement makes the selection of a bond very conservative because it ensures debentures (unsecured debt), and other miscellaneous items are accounted for. It's important to remember that this regulation was only for public utility companies.

Equity Test of Doubtful Merit in the Case of Utilities. Graham expresses his concern over the advantage one gains by employing the 2 part test that the NYSB uses. He states that many of the figures used on the balance sheets were not reliable during his era. He feels the test should be used if the earnings of the company are unreliable. In such cases, the analyst may want to increase the standards for test (1) to 75% the property value, and increase the standards for test (2) to cover three times the capital stock.

Importance of a Real-value Coverage behind a Bond Issue. Again, Graham raises his concern for the reliability of book value figures for fixed assets. He encourages the analyst to ensure the "going concern value" (or market price if the company could be sold as a whole unit) is substantially higher than the funded debt. He really challenges the analyst to look at the value of the business itself instead of the value of its individual pieces.

Going-concern Value and Earning Power. In this section Graham describes the common belief that a company's earnings power is the primary method of valuing a business. He states that all other considerations are qualitative factors. He then cautions the reader from developing a single criteria for assessing the safety of a bond.

Shareholders' Equity Measured by Market Value of Stock Issues—a Supplemental Test. In an effort to determine the going-concern value of a company's stock, Graham reluctantly suggests the best method is using the current market price of the company. Quickly after this suggestion, he states that this is by no means an admission that the market price is anyway related to the stock's intrinsic value. Instead, its purpose is only to test if substantial equity is behind the company's total debt. This comparison or ratio would be the market price divided by the bonded debt. Graham then states that a company that has a large market price compared to its total debt is far safer than a company that has a lower market price that closely resembles its total debt. A demonstration of how to calculate this ratio is provided in Chapter 15.

Minima for the Stock-equity Test. At the conclusion of this section, Graham provides a chart that captures the intent of his text more clearly. The chart shows the three primary enterprises of his era: public utilities, railroads, and industrials. After each enterprise, he shows the minimum interest coverage that a company in each enterprise should carry: Earnings should be 1.75 times the interest of the debt for Public utilities, 2 times for Railroads, and 3 times for Industrials. Then, the next column demonstrates a test for the coverage for the principal on the debt. This column shows that the market price of the stock should be at least 50% of the total debt for public utilities, 66% for

Railroads, and 100% for industrials. Remember, these tests were developed for determining the safety of a bond, not the common stock.

Income Bonds Equivalent to Stock Equity. Since interest on income bonds (issues that aren't required to pay coupons) is not a fixed charge, it should not be included in the total charges on which coverage is calculated. Similarly, the principal amount of such bonds is not to be included in the total funded debt; instead it is to be compared with the stock equity.

Significance of Unusually Large Stock-value Ratio. As we now know, the consideration of a bond's security is primarily based on its coverage ratio (earnings compared to fixed interest charges) and its ratio of stock value to total bonded debt. The first ratio provides coverage of the coupon payment and the second ratio ensures the par value can be repaid. When either one of these ratios are uncharacteristically high while the other is low, it's possible that the issue is still safe. The analyst must employ sound judgment and make wise assumptions in order to understand how the debt obligation can still be repaid without delay or trouble.

Significance of a Subnormal Stock-value Ratio. Looking at the previous topic from the opposite perspective, Graham cautions analysts from accepting a security that has a low stock value to total bonded debt ratio. To demonstrate his point, he provides two examples. The first example demonstrates a company with a low stock-value ratio that ended up being called back by the company on favorable terms. The second example demonstrated a company's bonds that ultimately traded at a severe discount. Graham uses the two contrasting points of view to demonstrate that good or bad performance is difficult to predict when the stock-value ratio is low. In the end, this instability will likely jeopardize one's principal on the investment. He reemphasizes that the selection of bonds is a negative art. Graham suggests both issues should have been avoided.

Stock-value Ratio for Railroad and Public utility Companies. In this section, Graham warns the analyst that applying a stock value ratio to railroads and public utility companies is difficult because of rental obligations and preferred stock of subsidiaries that rank before the parent company's bonds. Regardless of those difficulties, Graham states that close attention to the stock-value ratio would have prevented major mistakes by bond investors in 1935-1937.

Stock-value Test Not to Be Modified to Reflect Changing Market Conditions. Graham acknowledges that many analysts might be inclined to make the stock-value ratio adjustable with changing market conditions (because it uses the current market price). For example, during a bull market, market prices are higher but the total debt of a bond is fixed. Therefore a ratio of 2:1 should potentially be increased to 3:1 during growing market prices.

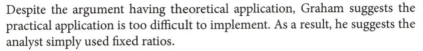

Despite the argument having theoretical application, Graham suggests the practical application is too difficult to implement. As a result, he suggests the analyst simply used fixed ratios.

Summary of minimum Quantitative Requirements suggested for Fixed-Value Investment

In this section, Graham summarizes all the quantitative information from chapters 8 through 11. It's important to note that the following recommendations were from the 1930's.

1. Size of the issuing organization: Municipal bonds should be from a local government with more than 10,000 tax-paying citizens. For businesses, they should produce annual gross revenues of $2 million for public utilities, $3 million for Railroads, $5 million for industrials.

2. Interest coverage: This is the comparison of earnings to fixed debt obligations. The seven year average interest coverage for each of the following enterprises are: earnings are 1.75 times the fixed debt for public utility bonds, 2 times for railroad bonds, 3 times for industrial bonds, 2 times for real estate bonds.

3. Value of property: The fair value of property should be more than 50% of the bond's par value.

4. Market value of the stock issues: This is a comparison of the company's stock market price to its total bonded debt. The stock price should be at least 50% of a public utilities bonded debt, 66⅔% of a railroad's bonded debt, and 100% of an industrial's bonded debt.

Chapter 12—Summary

Special Factors in the Analysis of Railroad and Public utility Bonds

Although many readers might be inclined to skip this chapter because it specifically talks about two narrow sectors applicable to the 1930's, the techniques and methods discussed are noteworthy. Graham separates the chapter into two parts; a discussion on railroad bonds and a discussion on public utility bonds.

In the first half of the chapter, Graham discusses the idea that profound research on high-grade bonds should be minimal. He demonstrates to the reader that their hard work and thorough analysis should fetch a higher yield than the same rate the investor could receive for a government bond. The chapter then transitions into the continued idea that a bond's coverage ratio and stock equity are the two primary concerns for determining the health of a bond. Graham uses the railroad companies to illustrate that countless amounts of data might be available to analyze, but all the information is of secondary importance to the coverage ratio and stock equity of the business. This chapter discusses the idea of holding companies and their subsidiaries. Graham provides examples how this corporate relationship/structure can be used to hide and produce earnings for short term reporting. The chapter also provides information for the speculative railroad bond investor.

During the second half of the chapter, Graham raises three concerns about public utility bonds. First he discusses his concern that many company's during his era simply use the term "public utility" to associate their business with stability, when in fact they might have little to do with the sector. Second, he identifies that many public utility companies use the prior deductions method for determining coverage ratios—Graham's deeply opposed to this method. Third, he discusses concern for the practice of omitting depreciation expenses from coverage ratios. Most of the information on public utilities is related to poor financial practices of Graham's era.

Chapter 12—Outline

Railroad-Bond Analysis

Like any kind of bond, Graham highlights the numerous variables that security analysts must consider when selecting railroad bonds. For this specific type of bond, three major areas need to be considered: The Company's financial aptitude, the value and quality of its physical assets, and its operational performance.

Elaborate Technique of Analysis Not Necessary for Selection of High-grade Bonds. In this section Graham suggests that the thorough analysis of high-grade Railroad bonds is not necessary. He further states that bonds of this type should be a simple decision for investors. If an investor is spending a lot of time determining the security of a high-grade railroad bond, he should seek a higher return than 2 to 4 %. Graham then suggests that the investor would be better off buying a federal bond because it offers a similar return without any of the concerns or effort/consideration.

Recommended Procedure. During Graham's era, it was easy for an analyst to receive a lot of information pertaining to railroads. Just because various amounts of data was available to the investor doesn't mean the information was valuable. Graham suggests that the analyst should ignore most variables and focus on the coverage ratio (Chapter 9) and the amount of stock equity (Chapter 11) for each company. If analysts seek more safety, they should increase the coverage on both of these two considerations instead of researching various pieces of other data.

Technical Aspects of Railroad-income Analysis. In order to conduct an interest coverage test on a railroad company, Graham cautions the analyst that it requires effort. He then describes how railroad companies often have various fixed charges and even fixed credits that persistently occur. The analyst must account for these additional items in their coverage test.

Methods of Computing Fixed-charge Coverage. Graham states that an exact science for determining all the fixed charges is not required. Instead, an emphasis should be placed on determining a reasonable accuracy opposed to an exact figure. Remember, the information is past performance and is being used as a guide for determining future performance. Graham then provides two tests for determining the earnings coverage for fixed charges. The test that provides the most conservative estimate is the one that should be used.

Test 1:

$$\text{Times fixed charges earned} = \frac{\text{Gross Income}}{\text{Gross Income} - \text{Net Income}}$$

For this test, gross income and net income can both be found on the income statement of the company being assessed.

Test 2:

$$\text{Times net deductions earned} = \frac{\text{Operating Income}}{\text{Operating Income} - \text{Net Income}}$$

For this test, operating income is the equal to the gross revenue minus operating expenses minus taxes. These figures are found on the income statement with the net income.

After providing these equations, Graham then exercises the tests with real companies from his era.

Bearing of Maintenance Expenditures upon Fixed-charge Coverage. Graham cautions the reader that a company's maintenance account can arbitrarily be determined by management. This account can be manipulated so earnings appear stronger than reality. This may impact future earnings negatively when management ultimately needs to disclose larger maintenance expenses. This potential issue can be identified by ensuring a consistent maintenance ratio is sustained throughout subsequent income statements. Graham then discusses the normal coverage ratio for Railroad companies during his era. The discussion covers the idea that maintenance costs were reduced as technology improved. Despite this reduction, analysts must remain vigilant in their understanding of why a reduced ratio might occur and consistently reassess their assumptions.

Nonrecurring Dividend Receipts. Graham highlights that it's important for the analyst to discount non-standard dividends paid by subsidiaries to their parent companies. These unpredictable payments often boost the earnings for parent companies when earnings are subpar. These sources of revenue should not be included when determining a predictable stream of earnings compared to fixed interest charges.

Excessive Maintenance and Undistributed Earnings of Subsidiaries. Contrary to the two previous sections, Graham quickly discusses the idea that some companies may take the opposite approach and overstate maintenance expenses and claim subsidiary dividend payments were not received. This method might be used to fool the security holder into believing current charges are overly conservative and future performance will be more favorable.

Analysis of Low-priced Railroad Bonds. For an investor interested in speculative railroad bonds, Graham identifies two key components: a deeper analysis of the road as a whole and the position of the individual bond.

> *A Deeper analysis of the road as a whole*—This section is further subdivided into two parts: the Character of Traffic and the Operating efficiency.

>> *Character of Traffic.* In this section, Graham goes into great detail describing the differences in railroad companies and their ability to competitive ship different types of freight. The discussion is very focused on current trends in the 1920-1930's. After the detailed discussion, Graham highlights that all the

factors he discussed are speculative in nature and likely doesn't assist someone in making an *investment judgment*.

Operating Efficiency. Graham lists numerous ratios that a railroad bond investor should analyze in order to assess the health of a speculative pick. For example, he discusses the operating ratio. This ratio is determined by looking at all of the operating expenses (with no tax) and dividing it by the gross revenues. This comparison will help the investor determine the efficiencies of the assets being employed for moving freight and any other operational actions. Graham makes an effort to outline all the variable a speculative low grade railroad bond investor should consider. Anyone deeply concerned with this specific kind of issue should read this section further.

The Specific Security. Previously Graham has stated that if one fixed income issue is postured for failure that all other subsequent issues are equally as dangerous. In this section he takes a slightly different approach for the speculative investor. He cautions such an investor that they better thoroughly understand the implications and priorities of underlying bonds and liens because the likelihood of a chain-effect failure is strong.

Public utility Bond Analysis

From 1926 through 1929, public utility securities greatly increased in America. During this increase, Graham felt the sector employed objectionable practices for issuing bonds. His reasons were threefold: 1) Industrial companies were slapping the term "public utility" onto their business in order to gain credibility. 2) The misleading "prior-deductions" method was being used to show the earnings coverage on their bonds (this was discussed in Chapter 9). 3) Depreciation was removed from the net earnings Calculation.

1. Abuse of the Term "Public Utility." Graham provides a discussion on what should or should not constitute a public utility company. From an investor's point of view, a public utility company should represent general stability. During Graham's era, companies that sold ice, operated taxi's, and owned cold-storage plants declared the public utility name.

2. Use of the Prior-deductions Method of Calculating Coverage. Please refer to Chapter 9 for a better understanding of the prior-deductions method and why its use is misleading to the investor.

3. Omission of Depreciation Charges in Calculating Coverage. Graham doesn't know how or why public utility companies did not included depreciation expenses in the net income figure used for coverage ratios, but he's of the strong opinion that the practice is unethical and misrepresenting the facts. At the end of this section, Graham provides an example of a company during his era that executed this technique.

Recommended Procedure. In this section, Graham continues the discussion of depreciation expenses not being included in public utilities coverage ratios. Since this practice was prevalent during his era, he provides numerous examples how the analyst could account for this oversight. In essence, if the company was reporting numbers that didn't include depreciation, Graham provides general guidelines for discounting net income by certain rates for certain industries.

Deduction of Federal Taxes in Computing Interest Coverage. In general, analysts should look at the coverage ratio for bonds before taxes are paid. Since taxes are determined after interest payments are made, the consideration of this expense (taxes) is not necessary. Graham then caveats this idea with the odd scenario where bonds are sometimes junior to preferred stock of subsidiaries of public utility companies. In this unique situation, the taxes expense on the dividends paid for the preferred stock would be deducted before the interest is considered on the junior bond. The whole discussion demonstrates to the reader how important a firm understanding of security prioritization should be.

Chapter 13—Summary

Other Special Factors in Bond Analysis

This chapter is of prime importance for any serious stock or bond investor because it lays out numerous considerations for the prioritization of securities. The start of the chapter focuses on the implications imposed on the subsidiary and parent company's security structure. For example, the preferred stock of a subsidiary out-prioritizes the bonds of a parent company. A thorough understand of this topic should be grasped by investors that wish to employ substantial capital in complexly structured institutions.

Graham closes this chapter with a brief discussion of working capital. He encourages investors to find companies with large levels of working capital because it displays a healthy organization that can meet future debt obligations.

Chapter 13—Outline

"Parent Company Only" vs. Consolidated Return. In this section Graham identifies his deep distrust for the parent company / operational subsidiary relationship—with respect to how the income statement is reported. He briefly describes and shows on a chart how the coverage ratio is drastically different when the income statement is viewed from the consolidated report to the "parent company only" report.

Dividends on Preferred Stocks of Subsidiaries. At the end of Chapter 12, Graham briefly discussed the prioritization of subsidiaries bonds and preferred stock. The discussion was in relation to whether taxes should be subtracted from the earnings coverage or not. Here, Graham discusses this prioritization further. Since parent companies are reliant on the dividends from the subsidiaries, those dividends actually out prioritize the bonds of the parent company. Below is the prioritization of issues for a company of this structure.

"1. Subsidiaries' bond interest."

"2. Subsidiaries' preferred dividends."

"3. Parent company's bond interest."

Etc..

This idea is based on the assumption that all the subsidiaries produce the same relative importance to the parent company's revenue structure. If not, further complications and considerations need to be accounted for. Graham then provides an example where a parent company fails and goes into receivership. Prior to the failure, the parent company had a subsidiary that was paying a preferred share dividend. After the failure, the dividend was immediately discontinued. The event left the bond holder (debenture holder) of the parent company empty handed. The example demonstrates an importance for thoroughly understanding the prioritization of this structure and an importance for having a backed security.

Minority Interest in Common Stock of Subsidiaries. The earnings of minority stock are usually deducted in the income statement after the parent company's bond interest, therefore it does not reduce the margin of safety calculation. Graham suggests subtracting the minority interest before calculating the interest coverage for a more conservative estimate.

"Capitalization of Fixed Charges," for Railroads and Utilities. Although many analysts may simply look at the fixed charges of a company's bonds as its sole obligations, Graham suggests further considerations are need for some industries. For example, the railroad industry may lease their railroad cars from other businesses. These leases hold considerable fixed expenses on the company and ultimately impact the health of the bonds the company has issued. After identifying this concern, Graham recommends a rule of thumb for multiplying the fixed charges on the income statement by 22. This would provide a capitalization of 4.5% on all the fixed charges. This was determined by taking the inverse of 22 (or $1/22 = 4.5\%$). It's important to note that interest rates for railroad debts during 1938 were 4.5%. Therefore, this technique could be applied to any industry where fixed charges have numerous variables. It would be important to adjust the capitalization rate based on the average rates for bonds in that industry. Graham then provides examples for two railroad companies and how this capitalization rate is applied.

The Working-Capital Factor in the Analysis of Industrial Bonds

Although the fixed assets on a balance sheet don't ordinarily carry much weight in assessing the health of a bond, Graham suggests the reader pay attention to the current assets. The current assets are the items listed on the balance sheet that represent cash or cash equivalents. Cash equivalents are items like inventory, which will soon be turned into cash when sold. These assets are common referred to as liquid, quick, or working assets. When conducting this analysis, it's important that a company has excess current assets compared to current liabilities. This excess is called the working capital.

Three Requisites with Respect to Working Capital. When assessing the working capital, Graham suggests three items should be evaluated. These items are:

1. The cash holdings are ample.
2. The ratio of current assets to current liabilities is strong.

3. The working capital bears a suitable proportion of funded debt.

Since each industry is different, Graham suggests that a fixed rule cannot be applied to each item. With that said, a general rule of thumb is that current assets should be double the current liabilities. Graham challenges the industrial bond investor to find companies that have enough working capital to cover all the bonds issued.

Graham concludes this section by stating that companies with a large working capital should be favored over ones without a large working capital.

Chapter 14—Summary

The Theory of Preferred Stocks

Although Graham has periodically mentioned preferred stock before this chapter, this is the first opportunity where he clearly defines his opinions on its role in financial markets. Graham makes no hesitation in identifying his distrust for preferred stocks. He claims preferred stock takes the least favorable element of bonds and packages it together with the least favorable element of common stock. Graham's greatest concern with preferred stock is the idea that management can immediately withhold future dividend payments with no reservation. Graham highlights other concerns such as the conflict of interest between common shareholders and preferred shareholders, the lack of voting rights for preferred shareholders, and the marginal yield an investor gains for the heightened risk of holding a preferred share over a bond. After outlining all of these concerns, Graham describes the very few scenarios where preferred stock ownership is suitable for an investor. He describes such instances as accidents by the issuing company. Graham concludes the chapter with outside sources that verify his opinion that preferred stock should be skeptically considered before purchasing.

Chapter 14—Outline

It should come as no surprise that preferred stock is an unattractive form of investment. The investor has no insurance on the principal of his investment and he also has no insurance on the payment of a dividend. Graham says preferred stock actually combines each of the limitations found in bonds and common stocks. With that said, preferred stock exists and needs to be understood by the analyst.

The Verdict of the Market Place. In this section, Graham provides a chart comparing the market price of United States corporate bonds, preferred stocks, and common stocks during the two major market down-turns on the 1930's. The chart shows the reader how preferred stock was most drastically impacted (negatively) by the poor market condition. Graham indirectly suggests this same scenario will occur in the future for preferred stock too.

Basic Difference between Preferred Stocks and Bonds. The major difference between bonds and preferred stock is that dividend payments on preferred stock is completely at the discretion of management. Therefore if management doesn't want to make a payment, they might not have to. Although bonds hold superior claim over preferred stock, Graham caveats this opinion with an interest quote. "If the company is good, its preferred stock is as good as a bond; and if the company is bad, its bonds are as bad as the preferred stock." As expected, this quote returns to Graham's general theme that great companies will produce great returns for the holder, but bad companies will perform poorly regardless of the priority of the security the investor holds.

Weakness Because of the Discretionary Right to Omit Dividends. When a company withholds dividend payments to preferred shareholders, it's very common to see the market price of the preferred stock plummet. Management will argue that the withheld payment is in the interest of the shareholder so those funds can be used for emergency purposes in the future, Graham has a tendency to disagree. Obviously the market sides with Graham point of view because the price drops when this practice is implemented.

Conflicts of Interest. In this section, Graham describes an interesting conflict of interest between common shareholders and preferred shareholders. Since the value of the preferred stock is completely dependent on the company's ability to make fixed dividend payments, the preferred holder has less interest in the overall long-term success of the business. This idea is in stark contrast to the common shareholder's point of view, because his success is based on the company's ability to grow and produce large earnings over time. Since most preferred shareholders don't possess voting rights, the interest of the common shareholder trumps their interests.

Form of Preferred Contract Often Entails Real Disadvantage. The investor should be prepared for the preferred stock contract to have severe disadvantages to the holder. To illustrate this point, Graham provides an example of the U.S. Steel Corporations Preferred Stock in 1932. When the Preferred Stock was issued, it was one of the largest issues in the world. The U.S. Steel Corporation had very strong performance and was expected to meet dividend payments without any hesitation. After the Depression, the company reduced the dividend and the market price on the preferred stock plummeted to two-thirds the issue price. In ironic comparison, the U.S. Steel Corporation had a 4.5% bond issue that didn't miss payment. Graham attributes this drastic difference to the weakness found in a Preferred stock contract.

Voting Rights a Potential Safeguard but Generally Ineffective. Although it would make sense for the preferred shareholder to gain voting rights if the dividend is suspended, this does not occur. As a result, the preferred stockholder has no control over the vested interest of his investment if management decides to discontinue the dividend payment.

Yield and Risk. Graham presents the argument that preferred stock's past performance has been so bad that it's questionable whether it should be considered a sound investment in the first place. Although a few examples of strong performance have been demonstrated, Graham revisits the idea that a higher dividend yield should not be used to compensate for increased risk. Instead, a discount on the stocks par value should be assumed when dealing with increased risk.

Qualification of High-grade Preferred Stocks. In this section, Graham outlines the requirements he uses for proper selection of a preferred share. First, the stock must exceed the minimum requirements that were discussed for fixed income bonds. This is required to offset the discretion management has to simply stop payment of dividends. Second, the company needs to demonstrate even more stability than the criteria described with bonds because that will likely provide the safety for a continued dividend payment.

Graham states that only about 5% of the preferred stock on the New York Stock Exchange in 1932 would have met this criteria. In order for a preferred stock investment to meet safety concerns, it should impose such a small burden of expense on the company that it could be carried no differently than a bond obligation. As a result, Graham suggests that a good preferred stock investment is likely the result of a mistake or anomaly on the part of the issuer.

High-grade Preferred Stocks Usually Seasoned Issues. Before the start of this section, Graham displays a chart of over 20 different preferred stocks during his era. Graham references the list and tells the reader that all of the issues meeting his criteria have performed exceptionally well for many years after the shares were first issued. Few corporations will sustain such an issue because they would rather recall the stock and issue a lower yielding bond and gain a tax advantage. The exception to this rule during Graham's time was public utility companies. This was likely because of the legal status of their bond issues.

Preferred-stock Financing 1935–1938. Although Graham feels preferred stock offers horrible options for investors, investment bankers may disagree. During his era numerous shares of preferred stock were issued to help finance companies.

Origin of the Popularity of Preferred Stocks. In this section Graham provides a brief history of why preferred stock was still popular in the 1930's. He states that prior to the first World War, many preferred stocks were trading for deep discounts. As conditions improved into the 1920's many of the investors holding these preferred shares benefited greatly as market conditions improved. Also during this period, bond-holders saw little to no growth on their investments. In a simple conclusion, many people developed the dangerous thought that preferred stock was more prosperous than fixed income bonds.

Poor Record Shown by Extensive Study of Preferred Issues. In an effort to prove to the reader that preferred stock in general is a poor form of investment, Graham references a case study by the Harvard Business School. The study analyzed over 537 different kinds of preferred shares from 1915 through 1923 and found on average that a 28.8% decrease in market price was experienced. This amounted to a larger decrease than the income bon- holders received during that period.

A More Recent Study. Here Graham provides a somewhat opposite opinion of the Harvard Business School, but with more refined variables. According to a study by the Bureau of Business Research at the University of Michigan, preferred stock performed quite well when it was not preceded by any bond issues. The section doesn't describe what constitutes a good performance.

Graham also highlights information from the same study that when a company's common stock performed well, so did the preferred stock. In obvious opposition, when the common stock performed poorly, the preferred stock performed similarly. Graham leaves the reader with the idea that preferred stock is clearly unwise in most conditions. Since preferred stock relies on the company's continued expansion of future profits, it lends itself to speculative features.

Chapter 15—Summary

Technique of Selecting Preferred Stocks for Investment

This chapter is a conglomeration of ideas that an investor must consider if purchasing preferred stock. The chapter starts with Graham's recommendation that stricter requirements are needed for preferred stock compared to bonds. Stricter guidelines are recommended because the analyst must account for the increased risk of management withholding dividends.

In the middle of the chapter, Graham provides a great reference for investors to calculate the stock-value ratio for fixed income securities. He provides this calculation to help investors avoid the potential mistake of determining the risk of a security by the prior-deductions method.

Next, Graham discusses the high risk of non-cumulative preferred stock. Under this type of security, management can legally withhold all dividend payments and pay no arrears for the life of the issue. Although this form of preferred stock is less desirable, Graham concludes the chapter with the idea that the company's performance and stability is the primary factor and consideration for proper selection.

Chapter 15—Outline

Graham reiterates his opinion from the previous chapter: Investment in preferred stock should meet the same requirements of a sound bond investment, plus an added benefit that accounts for the risk of management to withhold dividends.

More Stringent Requirements Suggested: Graham suggests that the preferred stock investor should require an increased coverage ratio over fixed charges. For example, when evaluating a bond, Graham recommended a coverage ratio of 3 times the fixed charges for an industrial company. Now, he suggests a coverage ratio of 4 times the fixed charges should be applied if considering the preferred stock of the same issuing company. In addition to larger coverage ratios, Graham also suggests that the minimum current stock-value ratio also be more conservative. For example, Industrial bonds required a minimum of $1 of bonds for every $1 of stock value. When considering a preferred stock of this same company, the bonds and preferred stock combined should hold $1 of value for every $1.5 of junior stock value.

Mere presence of Funded Debt Does Not Disqualify Preferred Stocks for Investment: Graham states that a preferred stock with no bonds ahead of it is obviously preferable. With that said, it's not required. Making a determination in how much bonded debt is ahead of a preferred issue is something the investor should pay close attention to.

Total-deductions Basis of Calculation Recommended: Graham highlights the importance of combining the dividend obligations of the preferred stock with the interest obligations of the company's bonds in order to determine the coverage ratio. The analyst must be careful to avoid calculating the coverage ratio separately because it would result in the same analysis as the prior-deductions method (learned in Chapter 9). This form of analysis is highly inaccurate and misleading. After this recommendation, Graham provides two examples of why investors should only consider preferred stock that's proceeded by small and manageable amounts of bonded debt.

"Dollars-per-share" Formula Misleading. Next, Graham discusses his frustration with the "Dollars-per-share" terminology for preferred stock. For example, $20 a share in earnings for preferred stock X. Graham warns investors that this type of terminology is misleading for the preferred shareholder because it fails to compare the earnings to the par value of the preferred issue. What the investor needs to understand is how much coverage the earnings have on the dividend obligation and par value of the issue. He proves his point by stating that $18.60 of earnings per share on 6% preferred stock with a par value of $10, is obviously better than $20 of earnings per share on 7% stock with $100 of par value.

Calculation of the Stock-value Ratio: Like the stock-value ratios discussed at the end of Chapter 11, Graham now teaches the reader how to calculate the stock-value ratios for bonds and preferred shares. Here's an example of how the math works:

Capitalization	Face Amount/# Shares	Low Price in time 2009	Value at low price
Bonds	$10,000	-	-
6% Preferred (1st issue)	20*	$100 par value	$2,000
4% Preferred (2nd issue)	150*	$100 par value	$15,000
Common Stock	6,000*	@ $20	$120,000

*Number of Shares

Stock Value Ratio for Bonds

Stock Value Ratio Bonds =

$$\frac{\text{Par Value of all Preferred Stock} + \text{Market Value of Common Stock}}{\text{Par Value of Bonds}}$$

$$\text{Stock Value Ratio Bonds} = \frac{\$2,000 + \$15,000 + \$120,000}{\$10,000}$$

Stock Value Ratio Bonds = 13.7 : 1

Stock Value Ratio for 1st Preferred Stock

Stock Value Ratio 1st Preferred Stock =

$$\frac{\text{Par Value of 2nd Preferred Stock} + \text{Market Value of Common Stock}}{\text{Par Value of Bonds} + \text{Par Value of 1st Preferred Stock}}$$

$$\text{Stock Value Ratio 1st Preferred Stock} = \frac{\$15,000 + \$120,000}{\$10,000 + \$2,000}$$

Stock Value Ratio 1st Preferred Stock = 11.25 : 1

Stock Value Ratio for 2nd Preferred Stock

Stock Value Ratio 2nd Preferred Stock =

$$\frac{\text{Market Value of Common Stock}}{\text{Par Value of Bonds} + \text{Par Value of 1st Prf Stk} + \text{Par Value of 2nd Prf Stk}}$$

$$\text{Stock Value Ratio 2nd Preferred Stock} = \frac{\$120,000}{\$10,000 + \$2,000 + \$15,000}$$

Stock Value Ratio 2nd Preferred Stock = 4.44 : 1

As one can see from the math, the level of coverage drastically decreases with the priority of issue. This demonstrates a plausible example of risk associated with each issue.

Noncumulative Issues: In this section, Graham discusses the terrible aspects of noncumulative preferred stock. When a preferred stock is noncumulative, management has no obligation to make dividend payments to the shareholder … ever. Whether strong earnings or weak earnings, the noncumulative preferred stock-holder has no entitlement to receive payment. This type of stock is highly risky to the holder and should be avoided if possible. Graham then discusses a lawsuit that was made in New Jersey against the ethics/ practice of noncumulative issue.

Features of the list of 21 Preferred Issues of Investment Grade: Here, Graham discusses the different and unique characteristics of 440 preferred stocks listed on the New York Stock Exchange in 1932. During this era, only 9% of the issues were noncumulative (today, the ratio is much higher. Also, hybrid preferred stock like trust preferred is available—which can defer dividends for 5 years). Although the different facts that Graham outlines in this section are interesting, the key point is that it's almost impossible to predict a preferred stocks performance based on its form, title, and legal rights. He demonstrates that non-cumulative picks sometimes perform better than cumulative shares. In the end, the most important aspects to consider are threefold: Find a company with 1) an outstanding historical performance. 2) a strong expectation for continued performance into the future. 3) an inherent stability.

Chapter 16—Summary

Income Bonds and Guaranteed Securities

In this chapter, Graham discusses the unique characteristics of income bonds and guaranteed securities. As previously mentioned, income bonds are different then standard fixed income bonds. These types of securities are often developed by companies during times of financial difficulty to produce cash and sustain operations. Since the focus of the income bond is to help the company continue operations, the terms of the issue are often unfavorable to the holder from the start. Income bonds often have a long term with unspecified coupons. Selection of income bonds should be treated with the same considerations as preferred stock.

In the second half of the chapter, Graham begins his two chapter discussion on guaranteed securities. A guarantee is nothing more than it implies; a guarantee by the issuing company, or an outside organization, on the coupons, dividends, or par value on a particular security. The most important part of this discussion is the idea that the guarantee is only as good as the issuer's ability to meet its obligation. The terms of the guarantee should be closely examined by the investor. Also, the investor should place more value on a guarantee made by multiple parties opposed to a single source.

Chapter 16—Outline

1. Income Bonds

Income bonds (also known as "Adjustment Bonds") are somewhat rare securities. They function as a mix between bonds and preferred stock. The only promise to the investor is that the par value of the bond will be repaid. The coupons are only paid at the discretion of management. Therefore, if the company isn't producing earnings or the bond is structured in a manner where capital expenditures are subtracted before an earnings figure is determined, no coupon payment may ever be made. Most income bonds also have a long maturity date. The income bond is commonly employed for corporations that are trying to avoid bankruptcy during times of poor financial health.

> **Interest Payment Sometimes Wholly Discretionary:** In this section, Graham highlights that companies issuing the income bond may have fancy legal rights in the indenture that allow them to fully avoid coupon payments. Indirectly, Graham suggests a close examination of the indenture of any income bond.

Low Investment Rating of Income Bonds as a Class: Graham highlights the idea that income bonds are often created under stressful financial situations for companies. Although income bonds might out prioritize preferred stock issues, income bonds are subject to payment only if earnings are available.

Increased Volume of Income Bonds Probable: During the early 1930's many companies experienced financial stress from the Great Depression. Since income bonds offered enormous tax advantages over preferred stock, Graham expected the number of income bonds to increase throughout the era.

Calculation of Margins of Safety for Income Bonds: Graham suggests that the analysis and risk calculations used for preferred stock is the same methods one should use for income bonds. Graham then provides an example of the calculations for an income bond. The example and calculations heavily discuss implications of ownership during the early 1930's.

Senior Income Bonds: Graham provides a few examples of companies that issued income bonds ahead of fixed income bonds. This section was provided as a mere highlight to the reader.

2. GUARANTEED ISSUES

An investor must be careful when accepting a "guaranteed issue". Graham discusses the idea that a guarantee is only as good as the organization that issues it.

Status of Guaranteed Issues: If a company guarantees the interest, dividend, or principal on any security, the company will be eligible for insolvency (the company will need to sell assets to produce cash) if it doesn't meet its obligations. If a security has a guaranty, it's likely to add to its safety. If the organization issuing the guarantee is in poor financial position, this should not negatively impact the security that's being guaranteed; instead it should be assumed the guarantee is worthless. A common stock or preferred stock that is fully guaranteed by another company has the same status as a bond issue for that guaranteer's books.

Exact Terms of Guarantee Are Important: Obviously, the terms of the guarantee are very important. A guarantee of principal and interest is far more superior then an interest only guarantee. To demonstrate an obscure example, Graham talks about a preferred stock (issued by Pratt and Whitney) that had guaranteed dividends. The company that guaranteed the dividends was called Niles. In the terms of the guarantee, Nile stated they would only guarantee the dividends if they had sufficient earnings of their own to cover the payment on Pratt and Whitney. Without surprise,

Pratt and Whitney, stopped paying their dividend on the preferred stock, and Nile claimed they didn't have sufficient earnings to cover the guarantee. Even more amazing, Nile continued to pay the dividends on its own preferred stock before arriving at the earnings figure that wasn't suitable to prompt payment on the guarantee with Pratt and Whitney.

Joint and Several Guarantees: When more than one organization is involved in providing a guarantee, special advantages are gained by the holder of the guarantee. Similar to having a co-signer on a credit card, both parties are responsible for the debts incurred on the card. With guarantees, if one party is unable to meet its obligations, those responsibilities are typically shared by all organizations involved in making the guarantee. Graham finds it odd that the market doesn't value such securities more favorably despite the reduced risk of failure.

Federal Land Bank Bonds: Graham counters his opinion that joint guarantees are superior to individual guarantees with an odd exception: the Federal Land Bank Bonds. In this section, Graham talks about a very unique sector that has twelve banks that issue bonds on farm mortgages. The bonds are then guaranteed by the 11 banks not involved in the issue. Although the discussion is specific to the 1930s, it leaves the readers with a sense of Graham's firm understanding and objective point of view on the subject.

Chapter 17—Summary

Guaranteed Securities (Continued)

This chapter starts with a brief background of the real-estate market in the 1920's and 1930's. Graham uses this background to help describe the complex problems the United States experienced in Real Estate Mortgages and Mortgage bonds. Although mortgage bonds are backed by tangible property, the safety of such bonds is only viable if the value of the property remains constant or increases in value (which wasn't the case in the 1930's). Third party companies that guaranteed the mortgage loans proved useless as an over-abundance of defaults occurred all at the same time; demonstrating Graham's main point that a guarantee is only as good as the issuer's ability to meet its obligation.

Next, Graham discussed the idea that property leases indirectly act as guarantees on property loans. For example, if an apartment owner has mortgaged a building, but has tenants in the building that have signed leases, the mortgage on the building is indirectly guaranteed for the term of the leases. As one might suspect, the terms of the lease and duration of the contract have an enormous impact on the quality of the guarantee.

Transitioning from guarantees, Graham looks at the idea from the perspective of the company paying the lease. When an analyst is determining the fixed charges for a company that leases its property, those fixed charges need to be consolidated and placed in front of the preferred and common stock of the business. These charges should be treated like coupon payments on bonds. Although leases are real expenses to companies, determining the coverage ratio for companies that heavily rely on such contracts is difficult to determine.

Graham concludes the chapter by discussing the idea that subsidiary bonds are not necessarily guaranteed by parent companies. The analyst must research the legal obligations between both organizations to see what responsibility the parent company has for its subordinate businesses.

Chapter 17—Outline

Guaranteed Real Estate Mortgages and Mortgage Bonds: Guarantees are most commonly found in the real estate industry, offered either by the corporation that sells the mortgages, or by the company that assumes liability for them. As such, they are a form of insurance for the holder of the mortgage, and will most commonly be successful if the mortgage loan is conservatively issued, the company issuing the coverage is large and diversified, and economic times are good.

This Business Once Conservatively Managed: For many years this business was conservatively managed, mortgages were limited to 60% of the property's value, risk was diversified, and the prudent companies survived the downturns prior to 1921.

New and Less Conservative Practices Developed: As the "new era" progressed in the 1920's many new business that insured the real estate mortgages grew from small town operations to nation-wide enterprises. Most of the loans made during this time were somewhat reckless and the companies granting guarantees on the loans where just as bad. When the market crashed at the end of the 1920's, the property values plummeted, and the loan companies and guarantor companies collapsed together.

The Effects of Competition and Contagion: By 1931, the real estate market had completely collapsed. Leading up to the event, it was common to see well established lending companies loosen their standards in order to compete with newly established businesses. After the collapse, it was obvious that the guarantee on loans was merely a title and nothing else.

Guarantees by Independent Surety Companies: Although it might be assumed that newly issued bonds with guarantees would be more secure because they had multiple organizations assess the risk of the loans, this was not the case in the early 1930's. Despite numerous surety companies (the companies providing the guarantees) providing this double check on loans, it still had no impact on the safety and security of loans. This idea goes back to Graham's comment about a guarantee only being as good as its issuer's ability to make payment. Needless to say, numerous surety companies went bankrupt during this era.

Leasehold Obligations Equivalent to Guarantees

The property of one company may be leased to another, and the rent paid may be sufficient to meet the property owner's debts. The contract that establishes this lease agreement acts in the same form as a guarantee. For example, if the person renting the property defaults on their payment, the lease then acts as a legal binding document for the property owner to collect on the renters obligations. As a caveat, it's important to understand the assets the renter owns before entering into a lease agreement. Graham provides two examples from the 1930's to demonstrate his opinion that lease agreements are equivalent to guarantees.

Specific Terms of Lease Important: Graham highlights the importance of thoroughly understanding the terms of the lease agreement. In a fairly complex example, Graham describes a Railroad company that had a 55 year lease with another railroad company for a certain line of track. Graham provides profound insights into the considerations an analyst must provide on the leasing company's bonds due to the contract. Some of the considerations were changes in interest rates, the changing value of the line of track, and possible prepayment on the grounds of convenience. The importance of Graham's example is to highlight the numerous variables one must consider if using a lease as a guarantee.

Guaranteed Issues Frequently Undervalued: In this section, Graham provides multiple examples from his era where guaranteed bonds traded for lower market prices (relatively speaking) than unsecured obligation of other institutions. As a result, he strongly encourages investors to consider the guaranteed issues over the unsecured ones.

Inclusion of Guarantees and Rentals in the Calculation of Fixed Charges

Here, Graham discusses the idea that some leases might be hidden or difficult to find on a company's balance sheet and income statement. This variable is of considerable concern for the investor. For example, if a department store leased it's building from an outside organization, the fixed obligations of the lease should be treated as a fixed bond ahead of the preferred and common stock.

Lease Liabilities Generally Overlooked: Graham highlights the idea that many long-term leases are not accounted for by analysts until its too late; most issues occur during poor financial markets.

Such Liabilities Complicated Analysis: It should come as no surprise that leases complicate security analysis. Since the S.E.C requires companies to report rent payments on the 10K (the annual report), the analyst should account for these expenses as fixed fees when determining a company's coverage ratio. Since the coverage ratios will be drastically impacted by lease agreements, Graham suggests alternate considerations: 1) only 1/3rd of the annual rental obligations (for building space) be considered with the fixed charges of a company. 2) The earnings coverage for retail stores should be reduced from 3 to 2. For preferred stock, the cover should be reduced from 4 to 2.5. Graham doesn't provide concrete evidence for the drastic decreases in coverage ratios he recommends. In fact, he refers to his own guidance as "Arbitrary and perhaps not the best that can be devised".

Status of Guaranteed Obligations: The analyst must exercise caution when making conclusions about the earnings coverage for a guaranteed obligation when the obligation and the guarantee both originate from the same business. As one can quickly see, a situation like this is not reducing risk because both factors are dependent upon same earnings.

Subsidiary Company Bonds

Although many investors might assume a parent company will offer protection on a subsidiary's bonds, this is not always true. In some cases, parent companies might not be contractually obligated to their subsidiaries. As a result, the parent company may decide to offload the failed assets of the subsidiary to its corresponding bond-holders. After describing this scenario, Graham provides multiple examples of companies during his era that executed this policy. The key point is that parent companies might not offer an indirect guarantee on subsidiary bonds.

> **Separate Analysis of Subsidiary Interest Coverage Essential:** Piggybacking off the previous section, Graham reiterates his concern for assessing the security of bonds in a subsidiary. He challenges the analyst to consider many variables when basing a position on guarantees. Sometimes a security will be priced in a manner that doesn't account for a guarantee, while other times the price reflects too high of a premium. When trying to understand the coverage of a subsidiary or holding company, always seek a consolidated balance sheet and income statement.

Chapter 18—Summary

Protective Covenants and Remedies of Senior Security Holders

This chapter is the start of a three chapter series on protective covenants for senior issues. In short, it discusses the legal documents and proceedings that occur with a business during bankruptcy proceedings.

To start, Graham begins with the documents that legally bind bond and preferred stockholders to the companies they invest in. These legal documents (often called indentures or articles of incorporation), set the standards for prioritization and ownership. These documents also describe the process that will be enacted in the event of a company's inability to meet payments to bond and stockholders. As mentioned in previous chapters, Graham reiterates his position that default proceedings (or receivership) on bonds and preferred stocks rarely return the principal to the investors. In an effort to describe the receivership process, Graham outlines the steps taken before and after 1933.

Throughout the chapter, Graham identifies problems with the current receivership process, but also provides recommendations on how the problems could be solved. Although some of the issues present in the 1930's don't necessarily apply to today's legal proceedings, the discussion provides historical reference for certain laws and procedures that still exist.

One of the key points for value investors was a short section contained in this chapter that discussed the variable trading prices of companies that are going through receivership. The section was provided to highlight the idea that the market will likely misprice assets in this vulnerable position.

Chapter 18—Outline

The goal of this chapter is to discuss the different types of provisions that are made to protect the rights of bond and preferred stockholders.

Indenture or Charter Provisions Designed to Protect Holder of Senior Securities: Like the start of any organization, a contract must be drawn between all parties involved. For bonds, this contract is commonly referred to as a "deed of trust" or "indenture." The contract for holders of preferred stock is in the "Articles (or Certificate) of Incorporation." The purpose of these documents is to establish provisions and actions that will occur during unfavorable events. At a minimum, these documents should address the following concerns:

1. For bonds:
   a. "Non-payment of interest, principal or sinking fund"
   b. "Default on other obligations or receivership"
   c. "Issuance of new secured debt"
   d. "Dilution of a conversion or subscription privilege"
2. For preferred stock:
   a. Non-payment of dividends over an extended period of time
   b. "Creation of funded debt or a prior stock issue"
   c. "Dilution of a conversion or subscription privilege."

The primary purpose of these clauses are to allow the holder to accelerate collection on their investment when the company doesn't meet its obligations.

Contradictory Aspects of Bondholders' Legal Rights: If a company fails to meet its obligations to a bondholder, the first inclination of the investor might be to seek receivership (a fancy way of saying the company needs to liquidate assets and payback the principal of the loans borrowed). Graham is hesitant to claim that this approach is feasible, reliable, and ultimately beneficial to the investor. Since the value of a company's assets drastically decrease in value when a company goes into receivership, Graham questions the viability of recovering enough funds to recuperate losses.

Corporate Insolvency and Reorganization: In this section, Graham describes the legal process of corporate insolvency and reorganization in the 1930's. During the time he wrote the book, legislation had changed due to the events of the Great Depression. As a result, his discussion first focuses on the laws prior to 1933 and then transitions into the newly implemented changes. In general, the process prior to 1933 during insolvency was the following:

1. The company was unable to pay interest or principal on debt
2. Selection of a court and the appointment of a receiver was made (typically the company's president)
3. Protective committees represented the bond holders (typically the banking houses that floated the bonds)
4. Reorganization plans were approved by the committees and the court; this usually involved a lot of flexibility and compromise from all security holders
5. A final reorganization was implemented; this was usually through foreclosures and bankruptcy sales. Graham highlights that most

investors were better off taking new securities in the re-organized business then holding-out for a cash payment from the liquidation sales.

The problem with this procedure was the former management often reorganized assets in a manner that was beneficial to them. The irony of this situation was management was the reason the companies experienced bankruptcy and re-organization in the first place. Laws after the 1933 attempted to fix this issue. The new laws placed more power with the trustee (who was an uninterested party), the S.E.C., and the judge overseeing the case. More emphasis was placed on the idea of ending the business instead of restructuring it under the same management that caused the failure.

Although Graham agrees with the new changes, he suggests voting power should be granted to the bond-holders immediately after receivership. This would allow the interest of the first tear capital providers to dictate the direction and organization of the business.

Tendency of Securities of Insolvent Companies to Sell below Their Fair Value: When a company goes into receivership, the value of its securities often trade in very odd and speculative ways. To demonstrate this idea, Graham provides optimistic example from 1932 of a company that had all of its securities trading on the open market for only one third of the cash in the company's account—not to mention the value of the other current assets and fixed property.

Voluntary Readjustment Plans: In this section, Graham describes the practice of a failing company's management to offering common stock to its bond holders in exchange for the termination of the bond contract. In one example, bondholders accept an 80% common stock position in exchange for $40 million dollars in bonded debt. In most cases, the value of the common stock after the exchange was worth much less than the par value of the bond, but the transaction prevented receivership in the short-term. Graham revisits the recommended idea of providing voting rights to the bond-holders for such a decision instead of allowing management to shape the deal.

Change in the Status of Bond Trustees: In 1939, a new law was passed to provide specific guidance and responsibility on the role of the trustee during receivership. Prior to this time, the Trustee would simply act as an indecisive and uninterested agent to the bond-holders of a failed company. His actions were rarely made on his own initiative. The new law, the *Trust Indenture Act of 1939*, charged the trustee with taking action and representing the interests of the bond-holders during such proceedings. The law also separated the conflict of interest that often occurred between management and the trustee.

The Problem of the Protective Committee: During Graham's era, the process of assembling a committee to represent the interests of bondholders during legal proceedings lacked standardization and regulation. Graham suggests major changes needed to occur to fix the injustices at such events.

Recommended Reform: Since the new *Trust Indenture Act of 1939* was recently passed during Graham's writing of the book (the second edition), he's of the opinion that the issues of representation may be fixed without further action. Graham provides an additional reform recommendation with the idea of creating a bondholders' group at the time of the bond's creation. This way, if the bond goes into receivership, an organized body is already assembled and prepared to issue its course of action. The organized body would have a non-participation roll in board meetings until a protective roll is assumed in receivership. The increased knowledge that this organized body would possess about the business would prove valuable during default.

Chapter 19—Summary

Protective Covenants (Continued)

In this chapter, Graham continues his discussion from the previous chapter on protective covenants for bonds. This chapter covers a host of topics that are deeply rooted in the different provisions and clauses of an in indenture (the formal legal agreement between the bondholder and company). Mostly, Graham raises concerns for unique and odd circumstances that an analyst must consider when buying or trading a security going into or through receivership. One common consideration is when a company is under financial stress, newly issued bonds may allow future issues to out-prioritize them. This tactic is typically used so management can find more capital if situations become worse.

Another common point of discussion in this chapter was the different types of coverage ratios that a company must sustain. These requirements are outlined in each securities indenture. Graham argues the practical applications of enforcing these ratios are difficult because it puts companies into receivership—thus complicating future performance and payment obligations.

At the end of the chapter, Graham discusses the application of a sinking fund. This type of fund is established to slowly repurchase the issued bonds of a company. The intent of the fund is to gradually reduce the company's liabilities on assets that may be decreasing in value. If a company is unable to meet the obligations of the sinking fund, or any other requirements in the indenture, Graham suggests voting rights are transfer to the bondholders.

Chapter 19—Outline

Prohibition of Prior Liens: When a company is operating under normal circumstances, it's very rare to find an indenture of a bond issue that allows newer issues to precede it. When a company is stressed and desperate for capital, an analyst must pay close attention to this matter. Likely, the company will remove this clause from the indenture so future capital can be raised. Graham provides an example of such an instance.

Equal-and-ratable Security Clause: When an unsecured bond (also known as a debenture) is issued, it likely possesses a clause that shares the value of mortgage liens that are later placed on the property. If this happens, the unsecured bond is somewhat secured by the property on the mortgage lien (note: the value of the property is shared across all previously issued debentures with the clause and the mortgage lien itself).

Purchase-money Mortgage: A purchase-money mortgage is when the buyer of a home or property doesn't have sufficient funds/credit to finance the entire purchase of a property. As a result, the seller relinquishes responsibility of their mortgage to the new buyer and the buyer pays the difference from the purchase price and mortgage balance to the seller. This situation is known as partial owner financing (even though the owner didn't lend their own funds). During Graham's era, it was common to permit these types of transactions without restriction. He argues this position may increase risk to the holder of the original loan.

Subordination of Bond Issues to Bank Debt in Reorganization: During the reorganization of stressed companies, it is common to see new bank loans precede previously issued bonds.

Safeguards against Creation of Additional Amounts of the Same Issue: Graham explains to the reader that most bonds are safeguarded against new issues by clauses that prevent management from issuing new debt without significant coverage ratios. He caveats this position with a discussion of the railroad industry and its lack of standards on coverage ratios for new issues. He concludes the discussion by stating that the practical applications of these safeguards are of little importance because future issues must possess attractive qualities in order to generate interest anyway.

Working-capital Requirements: Here, Graham discusses the lack of provisions on bond indentures for working capital requirements. Working capital is the difference between current assets and current liabilities. This section suggests that a minimum working capital requirement should be sustained by a company or else the bond holder gains special rights or the company must implement changes in dividend policies. Despite most bonds not having this stipulation, Graham says some industrial bonds did include the provision during his era. He provides multiple examples of such companies. In closing, Graham suggests that if the working capital goes below a certain threshold, the company should reduce or eliminate dividends paid to preferred and common stockholders.

Voting Control as a Remedy: As previously discussed, Graham readdresses his recommendation to allow bondholders to have voting rights during bankruptcy proceedings.

Protective Provisions for Investment Trust Issues: When investment trusts issue bonds to raise capital, Graham suggests the bonds should be treated differently than others. An investment trust is a company whose business is the investment of shareholder's funds. The shares trade like a typical public company. The most important consideration for an investment trusts' bonds should be the fixed excess of collateral that's maintained above the bond's obligations. If the value of the collateral should drop below the established threshold, more capital should be raised by shareholders or assets should be sold until the ratio is re-established. Graham suggests that investors of such organizations should demand this protective provision. During his era, standardization of this provision did not exist.

Sinking Funds

A sinking fund is an account that is established by a company to repurchase or recall its own bonds. The issuer makes periodic payments to a trustee who then retires portions of the bond issue by purchasing it on the open market or exercising the call option on the security.

> **Benefits:** From an investors' point of view, a sinking fund adds safety to the investment because the company is less likely to default on the principal of the fewer number of bonds still outstanding.

> **Indispensable in Some Cases:** Sinking funds are very important when the asset backing the bond is wasting in value. In theory, the depletion or depreciation allowance should be used for as an estimate for funds supplied to the sinking fund. Graham provides numerous examples of companies that had depreciating assets that were funded with bonds. A sinking fund gradually removed the bonds on the open market in order to reduce the liability from the company before the asset proved worthless.

> **Serial Maturities as an Alternative:** A serial maturity is a type of bond that matures at different times until the whole issue has matured. This type of bond is forced to perform a gradual repayment of par value (similar to the intent of a sinking fund) over time. These types of bonds are often used in state and municipal governments.

> **Problems of Enforcement:** Although most indentures have clauses that enforce the payment of capital to a sinking fund, Graham questions the practical application of doing so. As previous discussed, the impact that receivership has on a company and the value of its assets is severely detrimental to all parties involved. Instead, Graham revisits the idea of bestowing voting rights to the bondholders if payments to a sinking fund fail to occur. Graham concludes this chapter on protective covenants with a very important idea: **The success of a bond investment depends on the success of the enterprise and very little on the indenture.**

Chapter 20—Summary

Preferred-Stock Protective Provisions. Maintenance of Junior Capital

In this chapter, Graham discusses the same ideas and concerns of the two previous chapters, but now it is tailored towards Preferred stock. As previously discussed, a sinking fund promotes stability and sound management for repayment of principal on borrowed capital. When assessing the importance of a sinking fund for preferred stock, Graham argues it's even more essential. Similar to his suggestions in the previous chapters, Graham recommends voting rights for preferred stockholders if the company fails to meet dividend payments to cumulative and non-cumulative owners.

Graham concludes this chapter with a very interest discussion on the maintenance of junior capital. He provides numerous examples of how a board of directors (representing the common shareholder's interests) can issue new debt and actual distribute the proceeds from the loan as dividend payments to themselves (as common shareholders). The sneaky tactic is of considerable concern because it slowly transfers the risk of default from the common shareholder to the bond owners—all while the common shareholder retains control. The discussion is quite alarming and of considerable interest for any investors that invests in highly leveraged picks.

Chapter 20—Outline

Preferred stocks are almost always safeguarded against new issues being placed ahead of them. Although this criteria may exists in writing, the practical application is more ambiguous. If a company would face the issue of receivership, the preferred stockholders will likely find themselves in a very precarious situation. As a result, most preferred shareholders may choose to overrule this stipulation and vote for an amendment to allow new issues to precede them. Without this amendment, the company may fail causing the preferred shareholders to lose their entire principal.

Protection against Creation of Unsecured Debt Desirable. In this section, Graham describes the common practice of preferred stockholders having no control over the creation of debentures (or unsecured debt). The purpose of the exclusion was to allow management to fund typical operations with unsecured debt. The problem with the exclusion is it had no limitations on the size of the new issue. Graham suggests that secured or unsecured debt possess the same risk to the shareholders, therefore provisions need to stipulate limits on newly created debentures to protect the preferred shareholders.

Preferred stock sinking funds: The advantages discussed in the previous chapter for sinking funds are equally applicable to preferred stocks. In fact, since preferred stocks are in a weaker contractual position than bonds, adherence to a sinking fund is paramount. During Graham's era, few preferred stocks included provisions for a sinking fund. Despite the few companies with such provisions, Graham provides a few examples to the reader.

Voting Power in the Event of Nonpayment of Dividends. It's important to note that when a cumulative preferred stockholder does not receive a dividend payment, certain voting rights are typically bestowed upon them. It's important to note that this typically doesn't occur for the non-cumulative issues. To what degree voting rights are granted varies greatly from one preferred stock to another. In the reading, Graham provides four different examples of companies that missed dividend payments and the actions owners took to remedy the problem. Most holders gained voting rights after 1 year of missed payments. Graham highlights the important fact that most companies have a relatively small number of preferred stockholders compared to the common stock. In such cases, the newly acquired voting rights often have little impact due to a conflict of interest.

Noncumulative Issues Need Greater Protection. Here, Graham adamantly opposes the idea that non-cumulative preferred stock typically doesn't acquire voting rights when dividend payments are withheld. He argues that non-cumulative issues have an even greater risk and need for representation because the dividends can't be recovered. Although Graham doesn't feel a preferred vote should trump all common stockholders, he does think their voice should be represented regardless of the accumulation clause.

A General Canon Regarding Voting Power. Graham suggests that a general guideline should be adopted by all companies that allow voting powers to rest with common shareholders when dividends are promptly paid on preferred shares. When payments are withheld, Graham suggests the voting powers are reasonably shifted in favor of the preferred shareholders (regardless of the accumulation clause). This practice should be the norm instead of the exception.

Value of Voting Control by Preferred Stock May Be Questioned. In this section Graham describes a very interesting event where the Maytag Company (the makers of washer and dryers) issued large sums of preferred stock to the primary owners—the Maytag family. Once the family privately owned the windfall of stock (issued by the company), they then sold the stock on the open market for $20,000,000 (netting all the revenues for themselves). The preferred stock, now owned by thousands of investors, had a clause that transferred voting rights to the preferred stockholder if dividend payments were withheld. Needless to say, dividends were withheld and voting rights were bestowed. The importance of the situation isn't the fancy situation, but rather the lack of impact the voting rights had on changing the board of directors for the company. In the end, no one on the board was replaced. Graham provides this example to demonstrate how insignificant the voting rights might be for some issues.

Recommendation: In typical fashion, Graham recommends a fix to the problem. He suggests that the duty for resolving the problem should remain with the issuing house. The issuing house should be required to contact shareholders and advise them of their rights and options. Therefore the fix is providing education to the uniformed.

Maintenance of Adequate Junior Capital. Something that few bond investors consider when providing loans to companies is the power that common shareholders have to distribute the capital to themselves. In theory, a company could raise $1,000,000 through the sale of a junior bonds and immediately turn-around and withdraw the funds as a dividend to common stockholders. In this situation, the common stockholder transfers all his risk onto the bondholder while retaining control and voting rights of the company. The only way to guard against this behavior is to have strong provisions in the indenture (or contract).

Although the provided example is extreme and not likely to occur in this manner, Graham suggests companies perform this method of risk transfer all the time. Instead of the withdrawal of funds happening immediately, it's actually a slow and gradual process that occurs over time. To demonstrate the idea, he provides an example of the Interborough-Metropolitan case.

Graham warns the analyst that bond-holders are most vulnerable to this situation when management writes-down the value of assets. This action reduces the depreciation charges and therefore might allow a larger dividend payment to the common shareholders.

To protect against such sneaky tactics, Graham provides an example of a company that had explicit protection in the indenture for such cases. Primarily, cash dividends could only be paid from earned surplus or paid-in-capital funds. This criterion forces the company to earn money from the sale of a product before paying it to owners as a dividend.

In the final section, Graham describes the odd position that preferred stockholders have in this type of scenario. Although the preferred stockholder ultimately wants to sustain their dividend payment, this might only be possible by writing down the value of assets on the balance sheet in order to maintain certain earnings coverage. The conflict for the preferred shareholder is he also has a vested interest in maintaining an adequate amount of junior capital (or the equity that remains after all senior debt is paid off in full). By writing down assets on the balance sheet, the junior capital is reduced. As one can see, a preferred shareholder's thirst for dividends may negatively impact the company's ability to repurchase or redeem the issues at par value.

Chapter 21—Summary

Supervision of Investment Holdings

This relatively short chapter discusses the numerous types of investment services that are available to the general investor. The chapter begins with Graham's discussion on how the mind-set of the investor has evolved from a buy and hold strategy to a much more active and distrustful approach. Based on Graham's recommendation to consistently monitor the progress of an investor's portfolio over time, it seems Graham has adopted a similar belief and mistrust of the markets. This discussion of constant maintenance and re-assessment leads to Graham's suggestion: If a low yield investment is not trouble free, then invest in a government bond.

For the more serious and gifted security analyst, Graham implies a high profit can be obtained while still minimizing risk of principal. Although this approach can be applied, it requires great effort, knowledge, and focus on the part of the investor.

In one of Graham's more famous points, he has a section in this chapter that discusses margin of safety for fixed income securities. The dialogue is provided to demonstrate that the market price of the security will retain favor longer than a company with a lower margin of safety. This allows the investor time to react to the unfavorable movement and ultimately switch assets before the price is negatively impacted.

Graham concludes the chapter with a discussion of dealing with financial advisors. His primary highlight is to understand the interests of the advisor before subscribing to their guidance.

Chapter 21—Outline

Traditional Concept of "Permanent Investment": Graham suggests that prior to the 1920's, numerous investors sought permanent holdings. Their intentions were to find companies that represented stable and predictable returns that could be held forever. Then in 1922 a serious crash occurred and was followed by an enormous and prosperous bull market for 7 years (ending in 1929 with the start of the Great Depression). This boom-bust cycle drastically changed the innocent buy and hold approach.

Periodic Inspection of Holdings Necessary—but Troublesome: In this section, Graham voices his concern/frustration with the amount of effort one must exercise in order to select safe and sound fixed income investments. He states, "if a limited-return investment (something that's comparable to a federal bond interest rate) could not be regarded as trouble-free it was not worth making at all."

Superiority of United States Savings Bonds: After discussing the situations that had shaped the investing environment of the 1920's and 30's, Graham suggests most people were interested in three choices; 1) government bonds, 2) speculation, and 3) investments that protect principal and still offer substantial profits.

With respect to the first choice, Graham provides an enormous endorsement for the selection of United States Savings Bonds over almost all other forms of fixed income choices.

As one might expect, Graham is adamantly opposed to the second practice of speculation. He argues that ignorance, greed, and group thinking is totally unpredictable and likely to outbalance thoughtful considerations.

The third alternative is one that Graham would like to promote. He strongly cautions typical investors from this approach because they will likely lack the aptitude and knowledge to consider all the risks associated with certain picks. For the talented analyst, this should be their focus.

Principles and Problems of Systematic Supervision; Switching: It is very important for investors to systematically reassess their holdings at fixed intervals. This will allow them the opportunity to identify any issues before the market may react to the growing concerns.

Increased Sensitivity of Security Price. Graham identifies a term he calls "Price Inertia." This is the idea that bad or good news may drastically impact the stock price much more than the actual value of the news itself. For example, a company beats earnings estimates by $0.10. As a result, the stock price increases by $2.00 a share. The owner needs to be aware of this sensitivity and exploit its behavior to their advantage.

Exceptional Margins of Safety as Insurance against Doubt: In this section, Graham describes the practice of sustaining a sizable margin of safety and closely monitoring the company's progress over time. For example, if an investor purchased a company with earnings coverage of 20 and the standard protocol was only 3, the investor affords himself a handsome margin of safety. If however, that same company's earnings coverage was reduce to 4, the investor might be inclined to sell their position and seek something at 10 times the earnings coverage. The purpose of this approach is to allow the investor enough time get out of their investment while the market is still favorably pricing the security.

Policy in Depression: If the analyst is conservative in their selection of fixed income bonds, they will find the securities perform better than competitors' issues during depressed markets. This performance may offer the investor the opportunity to switch assets into a more beneficial position without paying a higher premium for similar or higher earnings coverage.

Sources of Investment Advice and Supervision: This segment tries to answer the difficult question: who should supervise an investor? The investor himself if he has time and knowledge, or employ an agent such as a broker or financial counsellor. The biggest concern for the investor is the self-interest of potential "experts". Since many investing banks have a specific set of securities they try to sell to customers, investors must remain leery of accepting such guidance. Graham provides a thorough discussion of the services rendered by commercial banks, investment banks, New York Stock Exchange Firms, the advisory departments' at large trusts, and independent investment consultants.

Part III
Senior Securities with
Speculative Features

Chapter 22—Summary

Privileged Issues

In this chapter, Graham discusses the mechanics of convertible, participating, and subscription based bonds and preferred shares. After each of these terms are defined (found in the lesson outline below), Graham discusses the advantages and disadvantages of owning privileged securities. In order to execute a sound strategy, the investor is encouraged to find convertible bonds or preferred shares that meet all the standard safety requirements discussed in Part II of the book. Once that type of security is found, the investor may benefit from owning a privileged version of the issue so the option to convert to common stock is available during time of high earnings. If the bond or preferred stock is convertible, its market price may automatically move in step with the common stock without having to convert the senior issue. More details on the math involved with this situation are provided at the end of the outline below.

Chapter 22—Outline

This chapter is designed to discuss the speculative features of bonds and preferred shares that have substantial changes in principal. The severe discount/premium at which these speculative securities trade are the result of 1) inadequate safety, or 2) special privileges or conversion features.

Senior Issues with Speculative Privileges

Three key terms are provided below to provide insight into key features that might make a security speculative.

1. Convertible: This means the bond or preferred stockholder can convert their position into common stock at a specified period in time.

2. Participating Convertible Preferred Share (PCP): This type of preferred stock is commonly used in venture capital (money supplied to start-up businesses by wealthy investors or organizations). A participating preferred share means the shareholder has a right to claim excess earnings (along with the common shareholders) in addition to the preferred dividend already being paid. This type of security can also be converted completely into common stock. This conversion is typically executed when the preferred shareholder realizes the business is producing growth and sustainable earnings that will yield a higher return than the dividend being paid on the preferred stock.

3. Subscription: This is when a bond or preferred stockholder has the option to purchase common shares, at a set price, at a fixed amount, and during a specific time.

Such Issues Attractive in Form: If a bond or preferred stock meets the requirements of suitability that were previously discussed in earlier chapters, and also has privileges (such as convertibility) attached to it, it's likely a desirable security.

Their Investment Record Unenviable: Reasons. Although privileged securities may appear desirable in theory, in practical application they have proven unsatisfactory. Graham suggests the primary reason for their marginal performance is the securities often lack suitability in their natural form. For example, the bond itself might lack a sufficient coverage ratio. In many cases, the privilege to convert the issue is offered to compensate for the weakness of the security in the first place.

A second factor is the vulnerability of the common stock price once a conversion has been made. If the investor simply converts their bond or preferred stock to common stock to materialize a sale and subsequent profit, this factor may not apply. But for the investor that converts their security into common shares and continues to hold the investment, Graham is skeptical of the common stocks' ability to continue adding value to the holder. To guard against this potential, Graham strongly encourages investors to view the new position from the perspective of the common shareholder—not as a fixed income investor.

Examples of Attractive Issues: Although Graham is skeptical of privileged securities, he also believes they can be purchased with reasonable success. To demonstrate these instances, Graham provides three examples from his era. In general, when the market price of the bonds/preferred shares are at parity with the market price of the common shares (meaning the value are equal), the investor may have a distinct advantage for owning the privileged security. This advantage manifests itself when the earnings expectations and general business posture is advantageous for common shareholder. Since the privileged security can be converted into common stock at any point (depending on the convertibility clause), the value of the bond or preferred share will likely follows the value of the common stock in lock-step as it's market price moves higher. Therefore, it may be more advantageous to not convert the asset to a lower priority form (i.e. common stock).

Example of an Unattractive Issue: After providing positive examples of convertible securities, Graham highlights a negative example with the National Trade Journals 6% convertible notes. Although this issue possessed similarities of the attractive examples (like the parity of the bond price and the common stock price), the bond's market value continued to deteriorate over time. Eventually the business went into receivership and the bond was relatively worthless. The learning point from the example was that the bond lacked strong coverage ratios and had inherent margin of safety problems during parity. These signs should have cautioned the conservative investor from risking the loss of their principal on the security—regardless of the privilege.

Principle Derived: In short, the investor of a senior privileged issue should view the investment from one perspective or the other; specifically, either as a fixed income investor or as a common stockholder. Graham says, "The investor who relaxes his safety requirements to obtain a profit-sharing privilege is frequently not prepared, financial or mentally for the inevitable loss…"

Rules Regarding Retention or Sale: Before discussing the rules for retaining a privileged security, let's first provide an example of how they work.

Let's assume a 5% convertible bond is issued at $100 par and is also trading on the open market for $100. The issue is convertible to common stock for the next five years at $25 a share. If the bond is converted to common stock, the holder will receive 4 shares of common stock in exchange for the bond. Presently the common stock is trading for $24.50. This situation demonstrates a parity of the common stock price and convertible bond price. If the bond holder would convert the issue to common stock, the value of his four shares would be $98 (a $2.00 difference between the common stock and the value of the bond). Assuming the bond-holder did not convert on their issue, the value of the bond would move in lock-step with the common stock if the security of the bond's coupons remained intact. For example, if the common stock rose to $30 a share, the market value on the convertible bond would likely progress to $120. This situation is where Graham makes his first recommendation to the reader. "In the typical case, a convertible bond should not be converted by the investor. It should be either held or sold." The reason for this guidance is simple. Why should the investor transition into a lower priority security when they are protected against principal loss and still have the opportunity to progress in value with the market price of the common shares. The variable that could potentially overturn this recommendation is if the term of the convertibility was about to expire or the bond was ready to mature.

Chapter 23—Summary

Technical Characteristics of Privileged Senior Securities

This chapter provides further considerations for the proper selection of privileged bonds and preferred shares. Graham starts the chapter by demonstrating the mechanics of a convertible bond. This demonstration is important because it allows the reader to have a foundation of how an investor could profit and identify risks associate with convertible issues. After providing this example, it becomes clear that the three variables behind the success of a convertible issue rely on the duration of the terms, the parity of the bond's market price to its common stock price, and the company's ability to grow its profits.

In the second half of the chapter, Graham briefly discusses the implications of a participating preferred stock. In short, this privilege allows the holder to receive additional dividend payments if the company becomes more profitable and makes larger payments to the common stockholders. It's similar to a convertible issue in that it allows the holder to share the profits of the business if conditions improve. Although convertible and participating issues allow the investor to benefit from the growth of a business, Graham warns investors that many businesses will attempt to recall privileged issues to prevent additional fees. In order to combat this risk, Graham highly recommends privileged senior issues with detachable stock warrants. An example of this type of security is provided in the outline below. With this type of security, investors have the ability to detach the profit sharing portion of the privilege from the bond or preferred share. This allows the investor to essentially hold two separate securities that both demonstrate individual value.

Chapter 23—Outline

In the previous chapter Graham discussed the basic fundamentals of convertible, participating, and subscription based senior securities. In this chapter, he provides more depth and understanding on the same ideas.

Considerations Generally Applicable to Privileged Issues

In general, a convertible issue allows a bond-holder the safety of a fixed income investment while affording him the opportunity to the profits of the business.

This advantage can only materialize based on the terms of the arrangement and the aptitude of the company to increase its profits.

Terms of the Privilege vs. Prospects for the Enterprise:

Let's assume we have two different companies with slightly different terms:

Company A

5% bond selling at $50

Convertible into two shares of stock at $25

Stock is currently selling at $15

Company B

5% bond selling at $50

Convertible into four shares of stock at $12.50

Stock is currently selling at $11.50

Based on the figures above, which company is more advantageous to the investor? Graham would argue Company B is more advantageous from a terms perspective because it only has $1.00 of price growth until the bond is at parity with the common stock. Although this might appear as the obvious choice, Graham's not so quick to declare one pick over the other. His opinion is that the company that has the stronger prospects for future growth is likely to be the better candidate. For example, Company B's stock price could remain flat with marginal earnings potential, while Company A could have very promising profit expectations.

Three Important Elements:

1. *Extent of Privilege.* It's very important for a convertible bond investor to understand the company's ability to grow its common stock price. In addition to this consideration, the investor will greatly benefit from a privilege that has closeness or parity between the bond's par value and the common stock's market price (like the example provided above with Company B). Finally, the duration of the privilege is important because it may only offer the conversion for a short period of time. If the privilege expires before the common stock conversion exceeds the value of the bond, the privilege holds no value.

   a. *Significance of Call on Large Number of Shares a Low Price.* Since low priced shares are more prone to fluctuate over a larger range of market price than high priced shares, the speculative value might be more beneficial if the security is at parity (the conversion from the bond to the common stock is equal).

2. *Closeness.* As previously mentioned, the closer a bond comes towards its parity in common stock price, the more attractive it becomes. The investor should be sure to include an assessment of the common stock's dividend expectations at the point of parity. Remember, the bond's value will continue to track the common stock price, so once a conversion has been made, the investor losses the safety of the bond's steadier market price.

3. *Duration.* An obvious fact is that the duration of the privilege must allow the convertibility of the security enough time to bloom. For example, if a bond is at parity with it's common stock price, but the privilege expires in 1 month, the investor has a very small amount of time to benefit from profit growth. Once that period is over, the investor would be unprotected from a price decline if the bond was converted into common stock.

Comparative Merits of the Three Types of Privilege. In this section Graham discusses the advantages and features of a participating feature.

In general, a participating preferred stock not only enjoys its own fixed dividends, but it's capable of receiving additional dividends based on predetermined conditions. Most likely those conditions specify that the preferred shareholder will get an additional dividend payment if the common stockholders receive a dividend in excess of the preferred stock's fixed dividend rate. For example, the preferred stockholder receives a fixed $1.00. After some time, the common stock has increased its dividend to $1.10. At this point, the participating feature would allow the preferred shareholder to also receive a $1.10 dividend.

Participating Issues at Disadvantage, Marketwise: Graham discusses the idea that a security's market price is likely higher if it possesses more volume. In the case of participating preferred stock, Graham suggests the issues will trade below their comparative pricing with common stock simply because of the low demand for the issue.

Relative Price Behavior of Convertible and Warrant-bearing Issues: When a company attaches a warrant to a bond, it allows the holder to purchase common stock at a specified price (like we've been discussing for convertible bonds). In some cases, companies will issue a detachable warrant. This means the holder of the bond can continue to own the bond and also exercise the warrant to own the common stock too. In the end, the investor would own both securities. A detachable warrant for the common stock can also be sold on the open market separate from the bond. This detached warrant would sell similarly to a call option. It's important to note that an undetachable stock warrant is also referred to as a convertible bond. Graham suggests that detachable stock warrants are more desirable and often trade at higher prices than convertible bonds (or undetachable stock warrants).

Advantage of Separability of Speculative Component: In order to understand this section, the reader needs a basic foundation of a stock option warrant. This privilege allows the holder of the option warrant to buy common stock at an agreed-upon price within a certain period of time. For example, if an option on company X can be exercised at a strike price of $12.00, and the current market price of the common stock is $20. Then the person executing the option will gain an $8.00 profit if the option is exercised and the shares are immediately sold. Since stock options are relatively cheap to acquire when initially placed on the market, there's often a lot of speculation associated with their value. If the $12 strike price for the option on company X was originally purchased for $2.00 per share (which is a fairly standard fee), one can quickly see how the value of the option would have changed from $2.00 a share to $8.00 a share once the market price reached $20. This background on stock option warrants demonstrates why the value of a bond that has a detachable common stock option warrant, often trades at higher prices than convertible issues. In short, the investor has the ability to greatly profit from the option's warrant if the common stock price increases beyond the strike price.

Second Advantage of Warrant-bearing Issues: One of the major drawbacks of privileged securities is the ability of the company to call the bond or preferred stock. This simply means the company can repurchase the securities at par value and take them off the market. This would inhibit an investor's ability to exercise convertibility to common stock once profits are starting to materialize. Although this setback might be true for convertible and participating issues, detachable stock warrants are unaffected by securities that are callable. As a result, Graham suggests detachable privileges are highly desirable.

Third Advantage of Warrant-bearing Issues: In this section, Graham provides the third reason detachable stock warrants are desirable: The investor can convert on the option's warrant to gain a quick profit, all while sustaining the ownership of the bond or preferred share. This dual benefit of not having to trade one security form for the other is much more beneficial than convertible and participating issues.

Chapter 24—Summary

Technical Aspects of Convertible Issues

The primary discussion throughout this chapter involves the idea of sliding scale convertible issues and unique considerations of privileged securities.

A sliding scale convertible bond or preferred stock has a changing strike price with respect to time. The intent of the sliding scale is to minimize the dilution on the common stock (if converted) as profits increase with market price. The dilution would occur as more common shares are placed on the open market from discount conversion prices. After describing the standard protocol of the sliding scale, Graham discusses the advantages and disadvantages of the privilege from the perspective of the bond and common shareholder.

The six final sections contained in this chapter provide rare examples of privileged senior securities that have non-standard features. The discussions serve more of a warning to investors of the numerous variables that exist when investing in these types of securities.

Chapter 24—Outline

If an investor is interested in purchasing a convertible issue, they must pay close attention to the technical aspects of the conversion privilege. In most cases, the terms of the conversion prices change as time progress. For example:

Company A

5% bond selling at a market price of $60 (par value of $50)

Convertible into two shares of stock at $25 from 1 January 2000—31 December 2000

Convertible into two shares of stock at $30 from 1 January 2001—31 December 2001

Convertible into two shares of stock at $40 from 1 January 2002—31 December 2002

Assume today is 31 December 2001 and the current market price for the common stock of Company A is $30 a share.

The first thing one should notice is the changing terms of this particular convertible bond. Although the bond is currently at parity with the common stock price, one could expect a drastic change on the market price of the bond if the investor waits one more day—1 January 2002. As time advances one day into the future, the bond is no longer convertible at $30 per share, but $40 per share. That price far exceeds the current market price of the common stock and therefore may propose an unlikely scenario for the common stock to exceed the $40 level within 1 year's time. If the common stock is expected to stay at the $30 price point, the convertible bond will likely return to its par value of $50 a share the following day. If the investor converts the bond into common stock today, they could realize the $10 gain by immediately selling the common stock on the open market.

Dilution and Anti-dilution Clauses: The value of a common share is considered diluted if the number of shares outstanding increase without a corresponding increase in assets and earnings power. This situation is commonly seen when companies issue stock options to their employees as bonuses. More shares are outstanding, but no new assets have been produced by the company. In addition to stock options, dilution occurs during stock splits and stock dividends. As we think about the implications this might have on a convertible bond or preferred share, it becomes evident that dilution negatively impacts the value of convertible issue. Imagine the example from the start of this chapter's outline. The value of the convertible bond increases with the growth of the common stock price after the parity price. Now picture the impact if the company continues to dilute the common stock price below the parity point. As a result, most convertible bonds have an anti-dilution provision that protects the holder, but such a provision is not guaranteed. Graham strongly encourages investors to be aware of the anti-delusion provision—especially if relying on the common stock price to exceed the parity of the conversion price.

Sliding Scales Designed to Accelerate Conversion: As one can intuitively determine, the purpose of a sliding convertible privilege is intended to protect the interest of the common shareholder. As time progresses, it's likely the privilege becomes less valuable to the bondholder if profits don't progress at the same rate as the sliding scale.

Sliding Scale Based on Time Intervals: Investors may feel the urge to convert their bond into common stock if a deadline on the sliding scale is approach (like the example at the beginning of the outline). This may prove to be a dangerous position if the common stock is held after the sale and the profits of the company deteriorate or subside.

Sliding Scale Based on Extent Privilege is Exercised: This section covers management's intent to try and convert the bondholders to common stock early in the term of the bond. Management may accomplish this effort by situating the sliding scale in an offset position that favors early conversions.

The move would encourage investors to realize the early profits and avoid the risk of losing the profit by retaining the privileged position. Management's motive for such an action would be to raise significant capital through the sale of the bond, while quickly reducing its debt obligations shortly after.

Issues Convertible into Preferred Stock: During Graham's initial days as an investor, convertible bonds that transitioned into preferred stock where quite common. As time progressed, he says the public realized the reward to transition into preferred stock was far more risk than it was worth.

Bonds Convertible at the Option of the Company: As one can clearly see, many of the privileged senior securities have countless variables that all impact the overall value of the investment. Graham warns investors that some issues are attractive while others are downright harmful and only have the interest of the common shareholders at heart. In one example, Graham demonstrates how a bond had the option to convert into preferred stock, which was at the company's discretion, not the bondholders. Gimmicks of this kind can exist and the investor must do their due diligence to avoid such risks.

Bonds Convertible into Other Bonds: In this section, Graham discusses the unique kind of bond that's convertible into other bonds. This type of security typically converts a short-term bond into a long term bond. Also, the conversion often places the investor into a long-term bond with a <u>lower</u> interest rate. This type of conversion privilege usually caries little value unless interest rates are uncharacteristically low (lower than the long term bond that it's being converted into) and the maturity on the original bond is about to expire.

Convertible Bonds with an Original Market Value in Excess of Par: In this section, Graham describes his disdain for a unique financing technique by a few companies in the late 1920's that issued bonds at prices in excess of their par value because of the subscription right to the common stock conversion. This was nothing more than a trick by management and the common shareholders to raise capital (from issuing more common stock) under the guise that the convertible bond had unique premium value.

A Technical Feature of Some Convertible Issues: In this section, Graham quickly mentions a very unique convertible bond that offered the option to purchase stock in exchange to the bond and a cash premium. The example is provided to demonstrate the various types of privileges.

Delayed Conversion Privilege: Although most privileged senior securities are effective immediately following their issuance, some are not. Instead, these unique privileges start after a specified period of time.

Chapter 25—Summary

Senior Securities with Warrants.
Participating Issues, Switching and Hedging

In this chapter Graham starts by saying most convertible issues have their counterpart in the terms of subscription warrants. A subscription warrant is the right to buy common stock at a fixed price and it's issued with a senior security like a bond or preferred share. Dependent on the detachability, the right to purchase might be, sold separately from the senior security. Here it is further found that an issue with detachable warrants will sell higher than one with non-separable rights.

To find the value of a participating issue the fixed payments earned should be included, as well as the right for distribution under the participating privilege. Graham further discusses that a participating issue on comparable terms might be more appealing than a common stock, as it offers both security and a chance for profit.

When facing a bear market a strong convertible issue will experience a less severe price decline than the common stock. This type of market might allow for making a profit by engaging in an opposite transaction of the convertibility of common stock. This process is called hedging. In continuation of this, Graham emphasis that hedging is not as simple and fool-proof as it might be perceived.

Chapter 25—Outline

Nearly all the variations found in convertible issues have their counterpart in the terms of subscription warrants. The purchase price of the stock is ordinarily subject to change, up or down, corresponding to the standard provisions for adjusting a conversion price, as Graham also discussed in Chapter 24.

Sliding Scales of Both Types. A sliding-scale arrangement could look as the following:

Example: Interstate Department Stores, Inc., 7% Preferred, issued in 1928, carried non-detachable warrants entitling the holder to purchase common stock, share for share, at the following prices:

> $37 per share up to January 31, 1929.
> $42 per share up to January 31, 1931.
> $47 per share up to January 31, 1933.

As with convertibles it can be seen that when the highest price is reached, it becomes an ordinary option purchase.

Methods of Payment. Stock-purchase warrants attached to bonds or preferred stocks frequently provide that payment for the common stock in either cash or by turning in the senior security itself at par. This method may prove directly equivalent to a conversion privilege.

Advantage of Option to Pay Cash. The option to pay cash instead of turning in the senior issue must be considered an advantage over a straight conversion privilege. The first reason is because the bond or preferred, "ex-warrants," may be worth more than par, thus increasing the profit. The second reason is because the holder may be glad to retain his investment while realizing a cash profit on its speculative component. The third reason is because the warrant is likely to sell separately at a greater premium over its realizable value than a pure convertible security. These arguments bring forth a further discussion on 'detachability'.

Detachability. Stock-purchase warrants are either detachable, non-detachable, or non-detachable for a certain period and detachable thereafter. A detachable warrant can be sold separately from the issue of which it originally formed a part. A non-detachable warrant or right may be exercised only in conjunction with the senior issue; i.e., the bond or preferred stock must be physically presented at the time of making payment for the common shares. In other words such warrants may not be added-in separately.

In an active stock market, detachability is popular with speculators, and they sell at considerable premiums above their immediately realizable value. The argument for making a warrant non-detachable is to avoid a very low price of the senior issue 'ex-warrants'. Speculators might be inclined to detach the warrant, and sell that off for whatever it will bring.

The compromise arrangement—which makes the warrant detachable only after an interval—is based upon the assumption that the security first needs time to become fairly well known in the investment world.

PARTICIPATING ISSUES

Most of the traits of this type of privilege have already been presented in earlier chapters. Two different participations are mentioned. The more usual arrangement for participation depends on the dividend paid upon the common stock; less frequently, the profit sharing is determined by the earnings without reference to the dividend rate.

Preferred shares constitute the majority of participating issues. Participating bonds are rare and likely to deviate widely in other respects from the standard bond pattern; i.e. how the payment to the bond owner is determined.

Privileged Issues Compared with the Related Common Stocks. In Graham's previous discussion of privileged issues as a class, it was pointed out that they sometimes offer a very attractive combination of security and chance for profit. More frequently, a decision may be reached that the privileged senior security is preferable to the common stock of that specific enterprise. Since such a conclusion is based on comparative elements only, it is likely to involve smaller risks of error than one that asserts the absolute attractiveness of an issue.

Note: It is very common for Graham's star pupil, Warren Buffett, to implement this approach. During deep recessions, you'll often find him purchasing senior securities with convertible privileges in fantastic businesses.

"Parity," "Premium," and "Discount." When the price of a convertible bond or preferred is exactly equivalent, on an exchange basis, to the current price of the common stock, the two issues are said to be selling at a parity (not to be confused with 'par' which is the face value of a security).

When the price of the senior issue is above parity it is said to be selling at a premium, and the difference between its price and conversion parity is called the amount of the premium, or the "spread." Conversely if the price of the convertible is below parity, the difference is sometimes called the discount.

A Fruitful Field for Dependable Analysis. When there is a senior issue convertible into common stock, the concentration of speculative interest in the latter often results in establishing a price level closely equivalent to (and sometimes even higher than) the price of the senior issue.

Conclusion from Foregoing. In general terms it is clear that the convertible issue selling on parity with the common stock is preferable of the two. It is also generally advantageous to pay a moderate premium to obtain safety of the senior issue.

Switching. As a practical rule, holders of common stocks who wish to retain their interest in the company should always exchange into a convertible senior issue of the enterprise, whenever it sells close to parity on a conversion basis.

The size of the premium paid for such an exchange is a matter of individual judgment. Because of the investor's confidence in the future of his company, he is usually unwilling to pay anything substantial for insurance against a decline in value.

But experience shows that he would be wise to give-up somewhat more than he thinks is necessary. This is in order to secure the strategic advantages that even a fairly sound convertible issue possesses over a common stock (all the possibilities of the common stock plus its senior position).

Hedging. Advantages of a strong convertible issue over a common stock become clear when the market declines. The price of the senior issue will ordinarily suffer less severely than the common, meaning that a good-sized spread may thereby be established, instead of the near-parity previously existing. This possibility suggests a special form of market operation, known as "hedging".

In the event of a long time rise in security prices, he can convert the senior issue and thus close the transaction at only a slight loss, consisting of the original spread plus costs incurred with the operation. But if the market declines substantially, he can "undo" the operation at a considerable profit, by selling out the senior issue and buying back the common stock.

Some Technical Aspects of Hedging. Hedging has numerous technical aspects which make it less simple and "fool-proof" than the brief description would indicate. Graham lists several arguments that the more experienced hedger should take into considerations, but also notes that a deeper discussion of hedging is outside the scope of the book.

An Intermediate Form of Hedging. An intermediate form of hedging consists of purchasing a convertible issue and selling only part of the related common shares, say, one-half of the amount receivable upon conversion. On this basis a profit may be realized in the event of either a substantial advance or a substantial decline in the common stock. This requires no opinion of the future course of prices.

Chapter 26—Summary

Senior Securities of Questionable Safety

In this chapter Graham investigates senior securities that are deemed unsafe. Examples could be low-grade bonds or speculative preferred shares. While the investor should not buy them, the speculator would often rather devote his attention to common stock.

While no quantitative selection criteria are described, important distinctions between senior securities with questionable safety to common stocks are made. In a few cases, having dividends has its advantage; arguments are presented in favor of carefully selected bonds.

Though Graham does not encourage engaging in securities with questionable safety, arguments for large working capital and low security prices, are suggested as components of evaluation. Finally three situations for mispricing preferred shares are provided.

Chapter 26—Outline

Graham starts out by presenting what he calls a "misfit category". That is the considerable part of the American securities which is composed by securities of questionable safety—for example, low grade bonds and low grade preferred shares. The reason why it is called a misfit category is because neither the investor nor the speculator, finds these securities interesting.

Limitation of Profit on Low-priced Bonds Not a Real Drawback: These securities are issued in large quantities and are held by a large number of people. The lack of demand will make for a price below intrinsic value, and the unattractive features *may* be more than offset by the attractive purchase price.

Two Viewpoints with Respect to Speculative Bonds: One viewpoint of the speculative bond is whether the lower price and corresponding higher yield will compensate for the lack of safety. The opposite viewpoint is if there is less risk involved with the lower price paid, there's no compensation for the smaller profit potential.

Common stock approach favorable. Graham suggests that the more speculative the security is, the more it needs to be analyzed like a common stock. Just as for common stock analysis the income statement and the balance sheet should be carefully examined to determine if the future is favorable or unfavorable.

Important Distinctions between Common Stocks and Speculative Senior Issues:

Graham will not set up specific standard of selecting speculative senior issue like he did with fixed value securities (Chapter 8-11), but certain distinctions to common stock should be presented.

1. *Lower priced bonds associated with corporate weakness:* Taking into consideration the fluctuations in the economy, the low price of a bond does not necessarily mean the company's future is going to be unsatisfactory. So at the bottom of the downswing it is possible for bond prices to recover as it is for the common stock.

2. *Many undervalued in relation to their status and contractual position:* Graham brings forward the assumption of a group of carefully selected low priced speculative bonds. If it is further assumed that the majority will survive and continue payment of their coupons. As a result, it will give the investors an advantage over common stock that is similarly priced.

3. *Contrasting importance of contractual terms in speculation and investment:* There is a distinction between investment and speculative qualities of preferred stocks. Compared with bonds, preferred stock's inability to enforce claim is a disadvantage. Compared with common stocks, preferred stocks are advantageous because of their probability of dividend payment.

Bearing of Working-capital and Sinking-fund Factors on Safety of Speculative Senior Issues: large working capital is an advantage to senior securities, when compared to common stock, because it ensures payment of interest and the ability to retire the bonds when due.

Importance of large net-current asset coverage: If the low-price bond is well covered by net current assets, the likelihood of repayment is good even though earnings may be poor or irregular.

Limitation upon Importance of Current asset Position: The importance must not be exaggerated. A bond that is fully covered by net current assets is not assured per definition. Current assets may be reduced by operating losses, or proved entirely undependable in the event of insolvency.

Speculative Preferred Stocks (stages in their price history): There is more irrational activity with speculative preferred stocks as compared to speculative bonds. Preferred shares may become mispriced, as shown in three potential stages:

1. *At issue, the investors are persuaded to buy the offering at a price which is not justifiable by the intrinsic value.*

2. *The lack of value is recognized. Price drops to speculative level, and overshoots in the drop*

3. *Price rises with speculation just as for common stocks. For instance dividend accumulation is overemphasised.*

Rule of maximum valuation for senior issues: Graham starts by stating the rule of "A senior issue cannot be worth, intrinsically, any more than a common stock would be worth if it occupied the position of that senior issue, with no junior issues outstanding." The reason is that the common stock represents full ownership of the business, thereby also the same value that lies behind both the preferred and the common stock.

Excessive emphasis placed on amount of accrued dividends: Preferred shares with large amount of accrued dividend have shown to be subject to manipulation on the price of both preferred shares and common stock. The reason for this is that when the public is in gambling mode, unpaid preferred dividends have been absurdly seen as a source of value for both security classes. By this logic a common stock with no unpaid preferred dividend ahead it, should be less attractive (even at the same price) because there is no plan to clearing up the accumulations.

Variation in Capital Structure Affects Total Market Value of Securities: In theory, the combined values of issued common and preferred stock should be equal to the capital-stock issue. In practice, they sometimes aren't because this division of capital may have an advantage over a single common stock issue. This will be further investigated in Chapter 40.

Part IV
Theory of Common Stock Investment — The Dividend Factor

Chapter 27—Summary

The Theory of Common Stock Investment

As one might expect, Graham's start to the analysis of common stocks is somewhat robust. He begins the chapter with a general declaration that common stocks are often speculative and purchased for profit motives only. In order to select common stocks that provide less risk with reasonable returns, Graham suggests a focus on stable dividends that are in excess of stable earnings. Also, investors should seek companies with book values that are similar to market prices.

Next, Graham provides a historical account of investing before the World War. According to Graham, investors of this era looked for common stocks that represented stability and conservative values. Investors often compared their investments to the value of bond coupons and looked at promises of future performance as speculation and gambling. Next, Graham discusses the drastic change of opinions that occurred after the War. The New Era Theory was one that shifted the previous approach to a more liberal and earnings centric emphasis. Under this new approach, investors were only focused on the future prospects and earnings momentum when assessing the potential value of common stocks.

After discussing the differences between the two approaches, Graham voices his concern for the later approach. He cautions the analyst that relying on past earnings performance, especially earnings that have grown exponentially over time, is a dangerous path. The danger is mostly rooted in the idea that it's an unstable pattern of growth that can't be sustained. When the engine that supplies the growth wears thin, the investor's principal will likely dissolve with the company's earnings.

Chapter 27—Outline

Graham begins the book's analysis of common stock with a strong caution: investment in common stock is often speculative and analysis may be inconclusive and unsatisfactory. With that declaration firmly established from the beginning, he discusses three premises.

1. Common stocks are of basic importance and of enormous interest
2. The owners of the common stock wish to know their value

3. Human nature often masks logic behind an endless cycle of greed for profit

Broad Merits of Common Stock Analysis: Graham suggests that if a random common stock is selected for analysis, the conclusions one can draw are likely speculative. With that said, Graham caveats this position with the selection of an exceptional common stock. For example, a common stock that has no debt, strong earnings, stability, a competitive advantage, a strong balance sheet, etc. In order to find such exceptional common stocks, Graham sets forth on a mission to identify new rules and principals from previous generations.

History of common stock analysis: Over the previous 30 years (from 1910—1940), common stocks have become more favored due to their substantial earnings and dividends. With more and more companies providing detailed financial information, investors have had statistical data to substantiate their investments. During 1927-1929, Graham says most investors neglected this analysis and simply purchased more common stock based on speculative greed for profit and prophecy.

Analysis Vitiated by Two Types of Instability: In this section, Graham suggests two types of instability will destroy the analysis of common stock: 1) Instability of tangibles aspects, and 2) an enormous importance placed on intangible aspects. To demonstrate his point, Graham provided the market price, earnings per share, and dividend history of four different picks over multiple decades. After showing the price movement, Graham made a general conclusion.

A company's market price was generally stable and predictable if the companies had the following characteristics:

1. The company paid a reasonable and consistent dividend
2. Earnings were stable and averaged a substantial margin over the dividend
3. Each dollar of market price was backed by actual assets of equal value on the balance sheet—Or in other words, the book value was similar to the market price.

Prewar (WW1) Conception of Investment in Common Stocks: Prior to the world war, the analyst was primarily concerned with finding common stocks that paid consistent dividends and possessed stable earnings. Other considerations were generally analyzed and used to discount the value as appropriate. In general, most emphasis was placed on past performance and little on future earnings growth.

Speculation characterized by emphasis on future prospects: When an analyst would rely on the improvement of a company's future performance to substantiate a premium on the market price, this idea was generally considered speculative. Since the future is uncertain, there's no way of actually knowing if the company possessed the aptitude to actually materialize expectations.

Technique of investing in common stocks resembled that for bonds: It becomes evident that investing in common stock is very similar to the techniques of investing in bonds. More specifically, common stocks are similar to the methods of investing in second-grade bonds. The lack of earnings coverage for the principal invested in common stock is offset by the chance of receiving a higher return on the dividend and market growth.

Buying common stocks viewed as taking a share in a business: Prior to the war, businessmen valued common stock the same way they valued an entire business. For example, if a businessman were going to purchase an entire company outright, he would likely start with the net worth of all the assets (or equity on the balance sheet), and then consider if the choice produced adequate earnings for the price. Graham discusses how this type of investor would look at the book value of the investment in the same light as the par value of a bond. After looking at the earnings that the company produced, the investor would decide if he was willing to pay a premium or discount to that par value (or book value). Therefore one of the jobs of the analysts is to determine if the assets represented on the balance sheet are actually worth their listed values. This section provides great clues into the methods that Benjamin Graham and Warren Buffett use to calculate the intrinsic value of common stocks.

The New Era Theory

During the roaring 1920's, Graham describes a unique shift in the way investors treated the value of common stocks. He says the change was primarily shaped by the new idea that the value of a common stock was completely dependent on what it will earn in the future. This new thesis had three supporting insights:

1. The dividend holds little emphasis on the value
2. The relationship between asset value and earnings power had little significance
3. The past earnings were of little significant value except when signifying momentum in growth

In order to assess this new philosophy of common stock value, Graham decides to discuss its causes, consequences, and logical validity.

Causes for This Changed Viewpoint: In short, Graham thinks the drastic change in common stock valuation stemmed from unpredictable results often seen from using historical data and the irresistible potential for profits that had occurred. Overall, the instability of the 1920's demonstrated a new economy where large stable companies often became vulnerable and small, unsuccessful businesses rose up to impressive earnings and dominance in the market. In the face of this instability, it should come as no surprise that the previous methods of finding solid companies with consistent returns were abandoned. Also, in the early 1930's many liquidations occurred. These events often produced very little value for the fixed assets the companies had listed on their balance sheets. This experience also caused investors to abandon the emphasis on book value or net-work of assets.

Attention Shifted to the Trend of Earnings: As one can see from the previous section, the approach for valuing common stock was abandoned. In its place was a new strategy that simply used historical data to estimate the earnings momentum of a company. This momentum could potentially produce growing profits to the holder.

The Common-stocks-as-long-term-investments Doctrine: Leading up to the stock market crash of 1929, Graham says a general theory that common stocks represented the most profitable approach for long-term investing. The theory was based on a few key points: 1. The value was based on what the common stock could earn in the future, 2) Good common stocks have a rising earnings (or EPS). The idea seems plausible, but what it excludes is the idea that a **price** is associated with the earnings one can expect to receive. Second, this approach relies on an improvement in the stock's future performance, therefore making the approach **speculative**.

New-era Investment Equivalent to Prewar Speculation: As Graham takes a closer look at the "new-era" approach, he quickly arrives at the conclusion that it closely resembles the speculative approach of the pre-war era.

Stocks Regarded as Attractive Irrespective of their Prices: In one of Graham's most blatant declarations in the book, he says, "The notion that the desirability of a common stock was entirely independent of its price seems incredibly absurd." To this idea, Graham proposes the following analogy. If stocks are trading a 35 times their maximum recorded earnings, maybe investors should look at the price in realistic terms. Would they be willing to pay $35,000 to earn a mere $1,000 return? That's what they would be doing when they buy a $35 dollar common share with only $1.00 of earnings per share (EPS).

Investment Trusts Came to Resemble This New Doctrine: Prior to the roaring 1920's, investment professionals operated in a sound and responsible manner. They focused on purchasing assets during depressed markets when prices were low. They looked to diversify their holdings and conduct statistical analysis to uncover undervalued stocks. Graham suggests these practices where sharply abandoned prior to the Great Depression.

Analysis Abandoned by Investment Trusts. One of the main reasons investment trusts adopted the new-era approach was due to the success they experienced during the 1920's without having to uncover detailed analysis. Graham voices his disgust for the professional investor who didn't safe guard the capital of their customers due to a lazy assessment of facts and risk analysis.

A Sound Premise Used to Support an Unsound Conclusion: In 1924, a book by the name of *Common Stocks as Long-term Investments*, by Edgar Lawrence Smith, was published. The premise of the book is that common stocks outperform bonds because not all the earnings are paid to the owners as dividends. This retained earnings by the company makes the value of the common stock increase in market price. Although Graham agreed with the basic tenants of Edgar's thesis, he strongly disagrees with the exaggeration many investors took in their application of his ideas. Instead, profit seekers made the unintelligent conclusion that if stocks outperform bonds, than any price can be paid to own them.

An additional concern was the massive emphasis investors placed on growing or declining earnings. To demonstrate his point, Graham compares the earnings record of three different companies. Company A had an earnings growth of 31% annually. Company B had an earnings growth of 7% annually. Company C had an earnings decline of 5% annually. After demonstrating these three different earnings scenarios, Graham showed the average price investors paid over the average earnings; Company A was 44 times earnings, Company B was 11 times earnings, and Company C was 7 times earnings. The analysis demonstrated that the new doctrine drastically favored the company with earnings growth.

Average vs. Trend of Earnings: In this section, Graham suggests that earnings trends and earning averages are nothing more than speculative tools for analysts to predict future results. In fact, companies that have accelerated growth demonstrate an untapped market for more competitors. Graham says, "the earnings curve will look most impressive on the very eve of a serious setback".

Chapter 28—Summary

Newer Canons of Common Stock Investment

This chapter serves as an overview of the selection of common stocks. Graham holds the opinion that an informed and disciplined investor can select common stocks successfully. This person needs to exercise severe caution and be very selective with each choice. In general, he suggests the stock market will continue to grow because of population growth and an ever expanding American Economy.

Graham then describes the practice of selecting "growth" stocks. As the founder of value investing, he's obviously skeptical of the practice and issues multiple reasons for his opinion. Namely, he doesn't think growth picks can be accurately identified, valued, or classified as investments.

Next, Graham discusses the idea of selecting common stocks that represent a large margin of safety. This is primarily obtained by purchasing stocks that trade at a significant discount to their intrinsic value. This approach can be implemented in two ways. First, the investor can purchase a group of stock when market conditions are experiencing turmoil and declines. Second, the investor can select individual issues that trade at a severe discount to their intrinsic value and provide strong outlooks for future performance. Although Graham doesn't specifically provide a formula for calculating intrinsic value, he discusses the idea of using a capitalization rate on the average earnings of an index (or group of stocks) to determine a normal value (explained more in the outline). This normal value is then compared to the actual market price to determine undervalued and overvalued times in the market.

Chapter 28—Outline

Although Graham's description of the techniques for valuing common stocks was quite negative in the previous chapter, he assures the read that proper selection is still possible. The way this is possible is threefold:

1. Have a diversified portfolio of common stocks
2. Use quantitative and qualitative factors to determine the value of common stocks similarly to the techniques for bonds.
3. Utilize even more effort than bonds to assess the future outlook of common stocks

Three General Approaches

Secular Expansion as Basis: Graham begins his argument for the future success of common stocks from a macro-economic perspective. He's of the opinion that the national wealth and earnings power will continue to develop positively. This increase will in turn reflect itself in the common stock market.

Through this natural progress, Graham suggests market fluctuations are bound to occur. When recessions occur, the investor can still benefit in the common stock markets by 1) diversifying their portfolio, and 2) by adamantly rejecting common stocks that trade for excessive premiums.

Lastly, Graham says the investor cannot rely on historical earnings growth to provide safety and profit in the long haul. Specifically, he's talking about companies that are commonly referred to as "growth picks". These types of companies have earnings that appear to be growing in an exponential manner.

Individual Growth as Basis of Selection: Graham discusses the idea of some investors that "growth stocks" are the most probable path to profit. Although some investors may be able to employ this approach successfully, Graham questions if everyone can do the same. To tackle this problem, Graham raises four questions.

1. *What are growth companies?* In this section, Graham provides a very vague and general definition of a growth stock; a company whose earnings move forward from cycle to cycle. A better definition might be one in which a company's earnings grow at a faster rate than the general market.

2. *Can the Investor Identify Them?* Graham would argue, no. He's of the opinion that the typical investor can't realistically determine when and where the company's growth will eventually subside. As a result, there's a strong chance that the investor might select the stock "at the top of the earnings wave".

3. *Does the Price Discount Potential Growth?* Graham suggests the most difficult decision facing the growth investor is the appropriate price to pay for future earnings that haven't been demonstrated yet. If the company is growing earnings at 30% a year, does that mean they should pay 30 times earnings? The question raises serious concern because it's impossible to predict how much longer the earnings growth is going to take place. One thing almost everyone can agree is that high earnings growth (like 30%) is temporary and not sustainable.

4. *May Such Purchases Be Described as Investment Commitments?* To answer this question, Graham issues a two part test. First, he asks if

thorough analysis and thought go into the selection of the growth stock. For this question, Graham says some growth investors do conduct themselves appropriately, therefore yes. Second, is the price paid for the investment something that a reasonable person would pay if they could buy the whole business? For example, would an individual be willing to pay $200,000 for a small business that currently produces $1,000 in earnings, but with 30% earnings growth from the previous year (this would be a P/E of 200)? Graham really doesn't answer this question, but he definitely treads in the direction of no. He says that if a person is willing to pay more than 20% more for a common stock than he would for outright ownership of the entire business, the pick become speculative.

Selection Based on Margin of Safety Principle: If an individual is considering the purchase of a common stock, they general have two courses of action. They can broadly buy stock during depressed market conditions or they can individually buy undervalued picks even when the market high. Depending on which approach one selects, or both, different factors must be considered.

Factors Complicating Efforts to Exploit General Market Swings. For anyone that looks at the graph of the stock market, it's easy to see it's drastic swings from high prices to low prices. So why not draw a line that splits the peaks and valleys down the middle and simply buy when the market is below the line and sell when it's above the line? Graham suggests that this method could be further refined and recommended if an index of leading stocks were selected and analyzed as a group (like the S&P 500). Also, a base or normal value for the group of stocks could be determined by taking their average earnings and capitalizing them at the going long term interest rate (like the 10 or 30 year federal bond). This idea is an extremely important recommendation for value investors. This is where Graham is telling analysts that the intrinsic value of stocks is directly tied to interest rates. For example, let's say the index has an average EPS of $10.0 a share. If the interest rates of the 30 year federal bond were 3.0% , Graham would recommend capitalizing the $10.0 earnings by 33.3. This capitalization rate is found by taking 1 divided by the interest rate. For example, 1 / .03 = 33.3. Therefore, Graham would suggest the normal (or base) value of the index is $333.33 at that particular point in time. This was determined by multiplying the average EPS of the index by the capitalization rate of 33.3. Once this baseline is established, Graham then compares the actual market price to this baseline. If the actual market price is below the base value, the investor can assume the index is undervalued. If the actual market price is above the base value, the investor can assume the index is overvalued.

Graham suggests this approach has three drawbacks. First, the general market patterns may be anticipated, but the actual buying and selling points may still be chosen poorly. Second, the market behavior may change in the future and not respond in the same manner as before. Third, this approach requires a very determined and vigilant individual because his actions will be the opposite of human psychology.

The undervalued individual issue approach: Graham suggests the likelihood of finding an individual common stock that possess the qualitative factors and the quantitative factors (compared to price) is rare. If this type of stock issue is found, Graham says it should be classified as an investment and not speculation. It is not hard to find a company that has favorable quantitative factors (a reasonable price compared to past financial performance), but it's difficult to find a company that has these features and also has very favorable future prospects. These types of business are likely to be found during intermittent periods of bad news or discrimination.

Graham says the most important way to view the purchase of a common stock is if the investor could purchase the entire business at once. This approach will always lead the investor in the right direction.

Chapter 29—Summary

The Dividend Factor in Common Stock Analysis

In this chapter, the reader learns some important opinions on the methods for valuing Common Stocks. First, Graham expresses his opinion that common stocks should be valued in a similar manner as bonds. Instead of valuing a coupon, Graham suggests the investor should value the dividend. Graham's main concern with common stocks is the company's method for distributing the earnings to the shareholders. Graham is of the strong opinion that a substantial portion of the company's earnings should be distributed directly as a dividend to the shareholder. For example, if a company has consistent earnings of $7 a share, $5 should be paid to the shareholder as a dividend. Graham thinks the higher dividend payment is more important than a lower and more consistent payment. His main reason for suggesting such a high dividend payment is because he thinks most companies' managements don't use the retained earnings to add more value to the shareholders. Instead the money is used as reserves for acquisitions (which proportionally add little value) or excessive salaries. Although Graham feels some companies can add value while retaining large portions of earnings, these businesses or far and few between.

Chapter 29—Outline

In a simple, yet important proclamation, Graham says the quantitative value of a common stock is based on three factors:
1. Dividend rate and record
2. Earning power (From the Income Statement)
3. Asset value (From the Balance Sheet)

Dividend Return as a Factor in Common-stock Investment: Although many modern investors look at common stocks differently than bonds, Graham suggests that the market price of common stocks will perform similarly if management pays a healthy and sustainable dividend. To demonstrate his conclusion, he shows two different companies over a decade's period that paid a consistent $7 and $6 dividend. During this time, the earnings of the companies fluctuated consistently (anywhere from $19.00 per share to $5 per share). Despite the constant change in earnings, the dividend remained intact, and so did the market price. Graham's point was confirmed by showing that the market price of the common stock reflected the actions of a bond with a similar coupon yield.

Established Principle of Withholding Dividends: If the management decides to withhold a portion of the earnings (the amount not being paid as a dividend), the theoretical reason is management is using the capital to benefit the shareholder. Graham claims that two companies with the same general business model and the same earnings will trade at different prices if the dividend policy is different. The market will value the company with the higher dividend more favorably.

Policy of withholding dividends questionable: Graham raises a very important question: Should a company pay a lower dividend in order to create stability for the owner with an assured payment, or should they pay a higher dividend and meet its obligation irregularly? For example, if a company's earnings fluctuate between $5 and $15 dollars a year, the average would be $10. Therefore, the ideal situation would be receiving an $8 dividend, while management retains $2 in surplus. This way they can use the surplus during years of lower earnings—or when the dividend exceeds the earnings. In practical application, this is not realistic. Instead the company might pay a $1.0 dividend for every $10 of earnings. Graham proposes the question, which technique is more beneficial to the investor? Through the rest of the Chapter, Graham attempts to answer that question.

The Merits of "Plowing Back" Earnings: In Graham's era, there were two arguments for why plowed back earnings (or earnings retained by the company) were beneficial to the stockholder. First, there was the opinion that whatever was good for the company was good for the shareholder. Second, a company that retained earnings had more agility to remain competitive in difficult markets.

Graham counters the first argument with the idea that there's a big difference between the interest of company owners and the company itself. For example, the company might like purchase a brand-new building with expensive glass walls. This expense, from retained earnings, may make the working environment of the employees better, but likely won't add value to the shareholder future income.

Graham states that a study performed during his era showed that companies with large levels of retained earnings did not generally expand their earnings proportionately. He concludes that companies that pay a larger dividend are more desirable than ones that don't.

- As an interesting, and ironic, side note, it should be highlighted that Benjamin Graham's star pupil, Warren Buffett, only once distributed dividend during his ownership of Berkshire Hathaway. Buffett has grown the company from $11.50 a share in 1964 to $160,000 a share in 2013. One of the reasons Buffett looks so closely at a company's return on equity (ROE; calculated by taking the EPS/Book Value) is to guard against the concern Graham raises in this section. In other words, if a company sustains a favorable ROE over a long period of time, it means the management is properly investing the retained earnings and adding value to the shareholder. If the ROE is deteriorating over time, it's likely the result of Graham's concern.

Dividend Policies Arbitrary and Sometimes Selfishly Determined: In general, there are numerous reasons why corporate management and the board of directors may want a lower divided rate. Graham suggests that many board members are executives and friends of executives with very large portions of shares. As a result, they might want to minimize their personal tax burden by receiving smaller dividends from the company. Also, leadership may seek a larger and more impressive sized business, therefore using retained earnings to fulfill their pursuit of an ever growing business (which may or may not add more earnings). Management may also seek the opportunity to purchase outstanding shares at lower prices with the retained earnings. This would essential use the money obtained by all shareholder (let's say 100 owners) and apply its value to the remaining shareholders after the buyback (now at 90 owners). Finally, a management that pays a small dividend is able to pay excessive salaries to executives and top level employees.

Arbitrary Control of Dividend Policy Complicates Analysis of Common Stocks: As a result of the issues identified in earlier sections, Graham concludes that it's extremely difficult to assess the value of a common stock when it retains large portions of its earnings and pays a small dividend.

Plowing Back Due to Watered Stock: Graham suggests the reason many companies in America were retaining large portions of earnings was to off-set the amortization of goodwill. Once the balance was offset by tangible assets—the retained earnings—the company had reduced their perceived risk and could reduce their levels of retained earnings.

- Note: the amortization of goodwill is no longer required; therefore this concern is not relevant in today's market.

Conclusions from the Foregoing: This section provides a glimpse into Graham's opinion on the value of common stocks. He says, if a common stock has an EPS (earnings per share) of $7.0 and pays a $5.0 dividend rate (the amount the shareholder receives annually); the stock should sell for approximately $100. Similarly, if a second stock had the same earnings of $7.0 a share, but only paid a $4.0 dividend rate, it should sell for $80. Graham determined this value by a simple comparison of the dividend yield. The first pick would have a 5% yield at $100, and the second pick would also have a 5% yield at $80. This simple comparison shows the reader that Graham placed little value (or was very skeptical) at valuing retained earnings power. He does caveat, this guidance with the idea that a company that has a larger earnings power but a similar dividend should trade at a premium. For example, if a third company had an EPS of $8.0, and a dividend rate of $5.0, it should trade at a premium of $100 because its ability to retain earnings is more likely than the company with a $7.0 EPS. This section is very general and does not provide specific rules for valuing common stocks with large dividends. The numbers provided as guidance in this discussion where assumed to be at normal market conditions (i.e. interest rates were average and stock market prices were average).

Suggested principle for Dividend Payments: Graham holds the strong opinion that a company should pay a large portion of their earnings to the shareholders. He says it's more important for the shareholder to receive non-standard (or inconsistent) dividend rates at a higher return, instead of a lower and more consistent dividend, which likely results in the company accumulating reserves that add little value.

Summary:

1. In some cases, shareholders can benefit from companies that have a small dividend policy. Although rare, these companies retain earnings and grow the net income of the company with the surplus.

2. More frequently, investors benefit from companies that pay a majority of their earnings as a dividend. Graham suggests that many companies that retain earnings are not doing it to grow their income. Instead the retained funds are used to sustain operations and it rarely adds proportionally to their earnings.

Dividend Policies Since 1934: In this section, Graham briefly describes a changing environment after 1934 where companies were distributing dividends at higher rates—especially companies that didn't have growth potential.

The Undistributed Profits Tax: In 1936, Congress passed a law that forced companies to pay a tax on retained earnings. This means if a company earned $7.00 a share (EPS), and paid a $5.00 dividend, the company would be taxed on the $2.00 it retained. The intent of the tax was to increase personal income so the country could generate more tax revenue. The tax was disliked by many and it was withdrawn within two years. Graham provides recommendations on how the law could have been implemented better. In the end, he suggests the choice to retain earnings should be at the discretion of corporate management and the shareholders—not government.

Chapter 30—Summary

Stock Dividends

In this chapter, the reader learns important lessons about stock dividends. Most investors are familiar with cash dividends, but stock dividends are slightly different and more difficult to understand. When a company issues a stock dividend, it's essentially dividing the company into more pieces and distributing those pieces equally to all the current owners. For example, image a pizza that has five slices. Behind each slice is one owner—therefore five owners. Now, imagine each slice is cut in half. The pizza now has 10 slices. Two slices are owned by 1 person. This is the essence of a stock dividend. The owners still have the same amount of pizza, but they now have more slices. When this happens to companies, the stock market values the division differently depending on how the slices are divided. In the pizza example, the owners would have received a 100% stock dividend. This is the same as a two for one stock split. In normal market conditions, the value of the company's shares would be split in half.

Although the stock dividend doesn't added more equity to the shareholder, it may allow the owner to receive more cash dividends in the future if the company sustains its current dividend rate. This is where the valuation of a stock dividend becomes more difficult for the analyst. Graham suggests a periodic stock dividend does add value to the common shareholder if the stock dividend and cash dividend is provided at reasonable and sustainable levels. In the outline below, examples are provided to demonstrate when these actions are appropriate.

Chapter 30—Outline

This chapter discusses the implications of stock dividends—a form of "payment" in the way of additional shares instead of a cash dividend. There are two types; extraordinary and periodic.

Extraordinary stock dividends are typically issued after a substantial amount of retained earnings have been accumulated over a number of years.

Periodic stock dividends are dispersed based on the current year's earnings. This is most likely the result of a company policy and likely to be repeated over a number of years.

Extraordinary Stock Dividends

A most common reason for the issue of an extraordinary stock dividend is to reduce the market price of the company. For example, if a company is trading for $500 a share, the company may issue an extraordinary stock dividend in order to increase the number of shares outstanding and therefore decrease the market price. In this scenario, if the company issued a 50% stock dividend, the market price would reduce to $333.33 per share. If the stock dividend was 100%, the market price would reduce to $250 per share. Since the extra shares are distributed equally across all owners, no real value is gained by any of the shareholders.

Split-ups. A split-up also occurs when the company issues more shares. From a valuation standpoint, a spit-up is no different than a stock dividend—it adds no value to the current shareholders. Its purpose is to add more shares outstanding and reduce the market price so it's more affordable. This is commonly referred to as a 2 for 1 stock split (or any other variation of numbers). A 2 for 1 stock split on a company that trades for $500 would reduce its market price to $250 (therefore it's the same as a 100% stock dividend).

Stock Splits and Stock Dividends in No-par Stock. The concept of par value for common stocks is often confusing for most investors. In some states, a par value for common stocks is not even required. In practice, par value simply shows accountants the original funds paid in capital to start the business. Regardless of the accounting rules and regulations for the par value for common stocks, it has no difference on the treatment of stock splits and stock dividends.

Objections to Extraordinary Stock Dividends and Split-ups. Although stock dividends and stock splits create no real value for the holders, much speculation about the value of the companies after the division is likely to occur due to the cheaper price.

Effect on the Cash Dividend Rate. Graham suggests it's common for companies to run-up a large surplus of earnings, issue a stock dividend (essentially splitting the shares), and then immediately increasing the regular cash dividend payments. The practice is adamantly opposed by Graham. He suggests management is trying to create speculative value to benefit their own self-interest.

Periodic Stock Dividends

As much as Graham disapproved of the extraordinary stock dividend, he holds an opposite opinion of the periodic stock dividend. The most noticeable difference between the two policies is consistency and predictability. With a periodic stock dividend, the shareholder often receives a smaller and reasonable stock dividend that adds value over time. For example, if a company earns $12.00 a share (EPS), and pays a $5.00 dividend, the company is retaining $7.00 a year in earnings. Graham suggests the company should pay a 5% stock dividend to help disperse some of the retained earnings. If the company sustains its $5.00 cash dividend during the next year, the investor who continues to hold their share (now at 1.05 shares) would receive a $5.25 cash dividend payment. The advantage of this policy is it often removes excess retained earnings from the balance sheet into the hands of the shareholders—assuming the dividend is sustained.

Variations in the Practice of Periodic Stock-dividend Payment. During Graham's era, the periodic stock dividend became popular. In most cases, companies did a combination of a cash payment and also a stock dividend payment.

Objectionable Feature of Periodic Stock Dividends. It's important to note that a company should not provide a periodic stock dividend if the amount exceeds the funds being retained in earnings. For example, when the company retained $7.00 in earnings from the $12.00 EPS, the investor cannot expect the company to sustain its earnings and equity if a stock dividend exceeds $7.00 and a $5.00 cash dividend is also paid. In the previous example only $0.25 was used from the $7.00 of retained earnings. This number is manageable and sustainable based on a company earning $12.00 in EPS.

Danger of Vicious Circle Developing. In this section, Graham provides an example of a company that paid a stock dividend that was too large. The dividend eventually exceeded the company's ability to retain earnings power and the EPS slowly declined over a ten year period—along with the market price.

Vicious Pyramiding on Stock Dividends. Here, Graham provides another example of a company that paid an excessive stock dividend that wasn't sustainable. Although the company was paying an unsustainable rate, the market still traded the company higher despite the artificial and temporary conditions.

Market Price of Shares Should Be Recognized in Stock-dividend Payments. During Graham's era, the New York Stock Exchange attempted to control the accounting laws of how company's received periodic stock dividends. The rule was set in place to address the concerns Graham described above. Graham suggests the law was in-effective because it failed to address the simple rule: a stock dividend cannot exceed the retained earnings while sustaining its future earnings power.

Advantages of Stock Dividends Payable in Preferred Stock. In typical Graham fashion, he provides a unique and thoughtful recommendation on how a company can disperse its retained earnings more effectively. Instead of issuing a common stock dividend, Graham suggests the dividend should be dispersed as a preferred share. This technique is suggested because it doesn't weaken the capital structure of the business like the common stock dividend.

This technique allows the company to retain earnings until a safe and manageable surplus is realized. Once this occurs, the company issues a preferred share as a stock dividend. That preferred share continues to pay the owner a new dividend until it's repurchased by the business at a par value. In the end, the initial common stockholder receives the value of the preferred dividend and its principal par value. This technique gives management flexibility and control to pay the dividend as long as they choose. Once the retained earnings have been distributed, the obligation is no longer on the books once the preferred share is repurchased by the company.

The Foregoing Summarized.

1. If a company is going to withhold earnings, they better have a good reason and process for doing so. Shareholders should demand a specific set of rules and regulations for retained earnings.

2. If a company needs to retain earnings out of necessity, the funds should be labeled "reserves" instead of "surplus profits."

3. If the company is retaining earnings, the funds should be distributed as additional stock periodically. The value of the stock dividend should never exceed the company's retained earnings.

Part V
Analysis of the Income Account — The Earnings Factor in Common Stock Valuation

Chapter 31—Summary

Analysis of the Income Account

In this chapter Graham emphasis why it is important that one does not solely rely on earning power found in the income statement (called *income account* in the original book). The income statement has more variability than the balance sheet, and since all funds flow through both statement, the analyst must refer to both.

Graham also presents a formula in two parts for determining the value of a common stock. One part of the formula is current earnings per share (EPS), while the other part contains a variety of factors determining the quality of the stock. This includes factors like the dividend rate, the size, the reputation of the company, the type of business and much more.

Words of cautions are advised when looking behind the earnings of the company. Using different accounting techniques management can manipulate earnings in the short run, and especially non-recurring and special items can mislead the investor that doesn't perform much research. Graham suggests that the great security analyst should resemble the work of a *shrewd and persistent detective*. That person can look through the accounting reports and locate the true earnings for the period studied and find indicators for the future earning power.

Chapter 31—Outline

In the past, investors would value a business through a holistic approach that involved analysis of a company's net worth (or equity) and also its earnings power. At the time when Graham was writing Security Analysis, he states that an over emphasis on earnings power has now been established. He's of the opinion that an analyst should combine the information from the balance sheet and income statement to garner the best valuation.

Disadvantages of Sole Emphasis on Earning Power: Graham finds it ironic that when an individual purchases a small business, they make considerations about the company's net worth (or equity) and the earnings power (or net income). In addition to this concern, Graham lays out other problems; the earnings statement has more variability than the balance sheet and therefore changes the value of the business making it appear unstable, the income statement can be more misleading than the balance sheet (assuming an investor with experience is analyzing the reports).

Warning against Sole Reliance upon Earnings Exhibit: Since all funds flowing through a business interact jointly between the income statement and balance sheet, an analyst must refer to both of these reports. Specifically, if the duration of the income statement is 1 year long, the analyst must view the balance sheet at the starting and ending point of the year.

Simplified Statement of Wall Street's Method of Appraising Common Stocks: Graham would argue that the standard "Wall Street" formula for determining a common stocks value is:

$$Price = Current\ Earnings\ Per\ Share\,(EPS)\ X\ Quality\ Coefficient$$

Now the interesting question for the individual executing this approach is how do they determine the quality coefficient? They will make the argument that the coefficient is determined by a whole host of factors. For example; the company's dividend rate and or history, the size and reputation of the business, the type of business, bull markets versus bear markets. Graham suspects all these factors are dwarfed by the real factor, which is the earnings trend. For example, if the company's EPS has grown by 30% from the previous year, the quality coefficient is much higher than a company that's had earnings decrease.

Earnings Not Only Fluctuate but Are Subject to Arbitrary Determination: After showing the reader that "Wall Streets" method for determining value or price is directly tied to the company's earnings (EPS), Graham provides examples of why that decision is such a dangerous path. In the short term, management can play accounting ticks to misrepresent the earnings during a specific period of time. In the long term, the truth will eventually arrive at the surface (either on the balance sheet or the future income statements). Some of the techniques management can use to misrepresent earnings in the short term are the following:

1. Through allocating items to surplus (on the balance sheet) instead of revenue.
2. Through misrepresented amortization charges.
3. Through an amendment of the capital structure.
4. Through the use of large capital funds for items that don't pertain to the business.

Significance of Foregoing to the Analyst: Graham suggests that a great security analyst will likely resemble the work of a shrewd and persistent detective. Their ability to uncover truths about the company's accounting will lead to their success. If the analyst uncovers a disguised truth, Graham cautions the analyst to act on the information gently. They should regard the information merely as an additional piece of knowledge about the company.

Placing extremely positions on a single truth may be a dangerous path. In the end, the analyst should be able to answer three questions:

1. "what are the true earnings for the period studied?"
2. "what indications does the earnings record carry as to the *future* earning power?"
3. What standards should be applied to the income statement to arrive at a reasonable valuation?

Criticism And Restatement of the Income Account

Graham suggests that few public companies are "cooking" their books—in fact companies have their accounts audited by independent accountants. Where the issue arises is the ambiguous way the accounting rules can be applied. This is where the analyst will need to pay close attention to the following accounts:

1. Non-recurrent profits and losses—this is a one-time or highly infrequent profit or loss. Note: In 2013, this is now referred to as extraordinary charges and is reported separately in the company's income statement at the bottom of the income statement after tax charges. As this is extraordinary, or non-recurrent if you like, it is *not* a part of the daily operations, hence the operating profit of the company would be overstated.
2. "Operations of subsidiaries and affiliates"
3. "Reserves."

Note: Accounting tricks with reserves can be executed in numerous ways and be labeled many different things on the company's balance sheet.

General Observations on the Income Account: accounting rules permit management a range of choices in recording non-recurrent and special items, selecting between *income* and *surplus (today also called 'gain')*; such items may be:

1. Profit or loss on sale of fixed assets
2. Profit or loss on sale of marketable securities
3. Discount or premium on retirement of capital obligations
4. Proceeds of life insurance policies
5. Tax refunds and interest on refunds
6. Gain or loss from litigation
7. Extraordinary write down of inventory
8. Extraordinary write down of receivables
9. Cost of maintaining non-operating properties.

It is arguable which is the "better" procedure to record such items, but they must be separated from the *ordinary operating results* in order that *indicated earning power* (what the company might be expected to earn if the business condition remained similar) is clear.

The report must also show any effects of subsidiary companies, probably in consolidated reports.

Reserves must be examined carefully since they may have been arbitrarily assessed by management, and over or under-recorded.

Amortization charges are another area of dispute in regard to how they are calculated and recorded.

Non-recurrent Items: Profits or Losses from Sale of Fixed Assets: these are not to be shown in current net income, they should appear in the surplus account.

Profit from Sale of Marketable Securities: must be separated from ordinary operating results.

Methods used by Investment Trusts in reporting sale of marketable securities: Prior to 1930 these were reported as regular income, and appreciation on unsold securities went into a footnote memorandum; in 1930 when there were large losses, these were shown as losses against capital, surplus or reserves, and unrealized depreciation in a footnote; arguably dealing in shares was their business and might reasonably be shown as business income or loss. Over-all changes in principal value are the only measure of an investment trust's performance, and this cannot be equated with recorded earnings of an industrial corporation.

Similar problems with banks and insurance companies: the funds of an insurance company are similar to those of a trust company; they have available for investment both their capital and the premiums paid in advance, and historically it has been the income derived that was what was left after claims were paid. Banks since 1933 have had to divorce themselves from affiliates and their restriction on permitted securities in bonds leaves them open to changes that mirror the bond market. An increase in the value of securities held by financial institutions should not be confused with or interpreted as "earnings power." But they have been and because of this they are not considered suitable holdings for the small investor.

Profits through Repurchase of Senior Securities at a Discount: a corporation may buy back its own securities at less than par value; any gain made is non-recurring and should be recorded as such. This was a feature of the Depression years 1931-33.

Other Non-recurrent Items: the remaining items on the list are regarded as inconsequential.

Chapter 32—Summary

Extraordinary Losses and Other Special Items in The Income Account

This chapter examines how accounting can manipulate the income statement. A discussion of write-down on receivables and inventory is introduced first. It is argued that expenses related to operations should also be treated as such, hence not as an extraordinary loss, which will overstate the operating results. Various techniques for measuring the value of inventory and the practice of accounting for deferred charges are also discussed.

Graham thinks that a more rightful approach is to spread out expenses at multiple years, 5 years is suggested. Both net income and operating income would thereby show a truthful picture.

Finally amortization (depreciation on intangible assets) on bond discounts is presented. Here Graham does not tell us his opinion on which accounting method to apply, but merely explains how and why methods have changed.

Chapter 32—Outline

While already established in Chapter 31 that non-recurrent losses have an impact on the income statement, Graham discusses if write-downs on inventory and receivable should be regarded as an extraordinary deduction on operating result. Many companies chose to do this in 1932 which was at the height of the Great Depression. As inventory losses are directly related to the conduct of the business, Graham suggests that it should not be treated as extraordinary.

Manufactured Earnings: Graham then brings up the example of receivables and inventory written down to an artificially low 'cost price', which in turn will lead to a manufactured higher profit in the year to come. This illustrates the most vicious type of accounting manipulation: taking sums out of surplus, and then reporting these same sums as income in the following years. The danger of this accounting method is the public is not likely to recognize it, and even the expert analyst might have a hard time detecting it. Graham rounds off this section by mentioning that most management is honest and that loose accounting is a highly contagious disease.

Reserves for Inventory Losses. Companies continuously set aside reserves to absorb losses on inventory before they occur. In the event inventory shrinkage actually takes place, it is naturally charged against the reserve already created. The implication is that the income statement does not always reflect inventory losses.

Other Elements in Inventory Accounting. The standard procedure is to take inventory at the close of the year measured by the lowest of either cost price or market price. The "cost of goods sold" is then found by adding that year's purchases to the opening inventory and subtracting the closing inventory value.

Last-In, First-Out. The first variation from this method consists of measuring the actual amount paid for the most recently acquired inventory. The theory behind this method is that a merchant's selling price is related mainly to the current replacement price or the recent cost of the article sold. This method may be useful to reduce income tax, if there is inventory fluctuation.

The Normal-stock or Basic-stock Inventory Method. A more radical method of minimizing fluctuations is the company must possess a certain physical stock of materials from year to year. This "permanent stock", would therefore keep the same value and not be imposed to any changes in price. In order to permit the base inventory to be carried at an unchanging figure on the balance sheet, the practice is to mark it down to a very low unit price—so low that it should never be necessary to reduce it further.

Idle-plant Expense. The cost of carrying non-operating properties is almost always charged against income—Graham suggests it should not. By doing so, it's misleading to the expenses of the company's core product or service. The analyst may properly consider idle-plant expense as belonging to a somewhat different category from ordinary charges against operating income, as these expenses by nature are not part of the company's normal operations.

In theory these expenses should be temporary since the management can terminate these losses at any time by disposing of the property. Therefore if the company chose to spend the money, Graham does not deem it logical to consider these assets equivalent to a permanent liability.

Deferred Charges. A business sometimes incurs expenses which are applicable to a number of years rather than a single 12-month period. Examples would include the following:

- Organization expense (legal fees, etc.).
- Moving expenses.
- Development expenses (for new products, processes, for opening up a mine, etc.).
- Discount on obligations sold.

The company is allowed to spread these types of costs over an appropriate period of years. The amount involved is entered upon the balance sheet as a deferred Ccharge, which is written off by annual charges against earnings. For many items the number of years may be arbitrarily taken, however, five years is a customary period of time.

Graham states it's common practice to write off these types of expenses in a single year, and against a 'surplus' (surplus meaning income from non-operating activities). This is incorrect, as the net income for the coming years would be overstated, followed from the understated operating expenses.

Most often the magnitude of such transactions is not large enough to have an impact that would lead the analyst to make an issue out of it. However, it does occur and Graham provides multiple examples to illustrate his point.

Amortization of Bond Discount.

Bond are usually issued by the company at a discount to par. This discount is a cost of borrowing money, and it can be seen as part of the interest burden. The discount should be amortized over the life of the bond by an annual charge against earnings. It was formerly considered "conservative" to write off such bond discounts by a single charge against surplus, as the company would show less intangible value among the assets on the balance sheet.

More recently these write-offs against surplus have become popular for the opposite reason, namely, to eliminate future annual deductions from earnings, and in that way to make the shares appear more valuable. This practice has aroused considerable criticism in recent years both from the New York Stock Exchange and from the S.E.C.

Chapter 33—Summary

Misleading Artifices in The Income Account. Earnings of Subsidiaries

This chapter is dividend in two main sections. First, Graham examines how misleading accounting practices can distort reported earnings. One method is to simply create earnings that don't exist, while hiding the accounting practices to the public. Graham suggests that one method to detect unsound accounting principles is to dig into tax calculations. He later gives the recommendation for the investor to shun securities have been exposed for improper accounting. Even if an adjustment still leaves room for a perceived margin of safety, he finds that no one can make a quantitative deduction when unscrupulous management is at play; the only way to deal with such situations is to avoid them altogether.

The second section looks into the earnings of subsidiaries. Graham provides examples of how parent company's can mislead shareholders when earnings are split among subsidiaries. Subsidiaries that are not consolidated are also prone to manipulation. One method is to let earnings accumulate in the subsidiary, and then pay special dividends to the parent company during poor years. Graham intelligently suggests that it's the duty of management to disclose the true earnings no matter circumstances and intentions.

In the end, Graham discusses the broader significance of losses by subsidiaries. These losses might be important for the profitability of the parent organization. After showing multiple examples on how earnings and accounting should be read by the analyst, he gives a general recommendation: if a parent company has an unprofitable division, its losses must be shown as a deduction from normal earnings.

Chapter 33—Outline

Flagrant Example of Padded Income Accounts: On rare occasions management would include earnings in the income statement that have no existence. A flagrant example of this was a company called Park and Tilford, Inc. The company wrote up goodwill and trademarks on the balance sheet by $1,000,000. Not only a big amount for the size of the company, but moreover these increases in intangible assets was deducted from the expenses during the same period they were wrote-up. This maneuver was presumably made to cover a reduction of $1,600,000 in net current assets.

Graham states that this is not only unsound accounting (these entries should have nothing to do with each other), but no statement relating to these deceptive entries was disclosed to the stockholders. Graham ends this section by noting that no accountants' certificate accompanied the annual statements of this enterprise.

Balance sheet and Income-tax Checks upon the Published Earnings Statements:

The example above illustrates why it is necessary to include the balance sheet when you analyze the income statement. This is a point that cannot be stressed hard enough by Graham, and he also finds it naive that Wall Street accepts reported earnings per shares derived simply from the income statement.

One option to check upon the reliability of the published earnings is to look at the amount of federal income tax accrued. The taxable profit can be calculated from the income-tax accrual, and this profit compared in turn with the earnings reported to stockholders. The two figures should not necessarily be the same, since the tax laws may give rise to a number of divergences. However, wide differences should be noted and made the subject of further inquiry.

Graham argues that this example points strongly to the need for independent audits of corporate statements by certified public accountants (which is the practice in modern times).

Another Extraordinary Case of Manipulated Accounting:

Graham presents another company, United Cigar Stores Company of America, who also engaged in unsound accounting and distorted earnings. Though the company disclosed the extraordinary accounting method of including "Appreciation of Leaseholds", Graham suggests the practice was still deceptive. Step by step, Graham discusses why appreciation of leaseholds should not be included in reported earnings figures.

Moral Drawn from Foregoing Examples: From the example of questionable accounting policies by United Cigar stores, it can be derived that all of it's securities must be shunned by the investor if detected. It does not matter how safe or attractive some of them may appear.

Graham cautions the analyst to not be enticed by companies with poor ethics despite a margin of safety that appears to exist. Such reasoning is wrong. One cannot make a quantitative deduction to allow for unscrupulous management; the only way to deal with such situations is to avoid them.

Fictitious Value Placed on Stock Dividends Received: Yet another example of manipulation with earnings is presented. This time, it was the United Cigar Stores, a subsidiary of Tobacco Products Corporation.

Detailed information about the company were not published, but earnings per share (EPS) were disclosed $11. To end up with this EPS number it could be found that approximately half of the earnings came from subsidiary dividend payments. While high dividend payments for holding companies are not unusual, in this instance it was almost 3 times previous levels. Graham discusses the implications on why it happened and how it was later forbidden by strict regulations.

SUBSIDIARY COMPANIES AND CONSOLIDATED REPORTS

The second general category of adjustments to reported earnings is in reference to consolidated reports. Consolidated reports occur when an enterprise controls one or more operational subsidiaries.

- Note: Consolidation simply means to cluster parent and subsidiary companies financial reports, and disclose it as a 'group' or one entity. Profit or deficit as well as the value of subsidiaries are in the parent company's books before the consolidation. The important part for consolidation is to ensure nothing is counted twice, for example, the profit of the subsidiary.

Former and Current Practices: Since passage of the 1934 act, all registered companies are required to supply subsidiary information either separately or jointly in their annual reports. Practically everyone follows the same procedure in their statements to stockholders.

Degree of Consolidation: Graham notes that even in so-called "consolidated statements" the degree of consolidation varies considerably, and different practices are used for each company and sector. One example is to only consolidate domestic subsidiaries, or to only consolidate companies that are fully operated and completely integrated.

- Today all subsidiaries that are controlled by the parent (typically by owning more than 50% of the subsidiary) need to be consolidated. The issues of manipulating earnings are illegal today.

Allowance for Nonconsolidated Profits and Losses: Graham describes various procedures for disclosing nonconsolidated profit and losses across different sectors. He suggests that the analyst should adjust the reported earnings for the nonconsolidated affiliates, if it has not already been done. He states that the criterion here is not the technical question of control, but the importance of the holdings.

Suggested Procedure for Statistical Agencies: Graham warns the reader about the oversimplification of common stock analysis with the single focus on earnings per share. Statistical manuals and agencies have focused on that, and he suggests the omission of such practices. He provides detailed guidelines for implementation.

Special Dividends Paid by Subsidiaries: Although parent companies can supplement their earnings through special dividends paid by their subsidiaries, Graham suggests this practice is not representative of the company's earnings potential. Instead the subsidiary is pulling from retained earnings to supplement the parent companies quarterly earnings. This can be very misleading to an analyst and they need to account for this in their evaluation process.

Distorted Earnings through Parent-subsidiary Relationships: Looking at the railroad industry, Graham provides two examples of distorted earnings through the parent-subsidy relationship. In one example, he shows a company reported a $5 EPS when in reality it was only about $2. A method of doing this is to "donate" money to the subsidiary (off the parent companies balance sheet), and for the parent company to claim back the same money as a dividend from the subsidiary.

Graham concludes that the result was no different than any other misleading accounting practices. It is to lead the public astray and to give those "on the inside" an unfair advantage.

Broader Significance of Subsidiaries' Losses: Graham starts this section by arguing that security analysis must allow for subsidiaries, despite the problems they can create for the analyst. He then posses the question; should a subsidiary's losses be represented on the parent company's earnings? Later he raises another question; should the analyst discount the value of the parent company if they own an unprofitable interest in another company?

He addresses the question above by referring to the discussion about idle expenses (from Chapter 32), and finds that these losses can be seen as temporary and thereby non-recurring. This is because the subsidiary can just be liquidated, hence should not be deducted as normal earnings. He then states that it is not an easy question to answer. Specifically, the lines get blurred because the subsidiary can provide an outlet for goods, or supply cheap materials, or absorb an important share of fixed costs for the parent company.

It may turn out, upon further analysis, that a good part of the subsidiary's loss is a necessary factor in the parent company's profit. Like so many other elements in analysis, this point usually requires an investigation well beyond the reported figures.

After this discussion, Graham provides multiple examples of when further investigation should be conducted. While no specific procedure is given, he gives the following general recommendation: <u>It is clear from the standpoint of proper accounting that as long as a company continues to control an unprofitable division, it's losses must be shown as a deduction from normal earnings.</u>

In the end Graham provides a short summary to avoid confusion:

1. In the first instance, subsidiary losses are to be deducted in every analysis.

2. If the amount involved is significant, the analyst should investigate whether or not the losses may be subject to early termination.

3. If these tests occur, the analyst may consider all or part of the subsidiary's losses equivalent to nonrecurring items.

Chapter 34—Summary

The Relation of Depreciation and Similar Charges to Earning Power

This is the first of three chapters about depreciation and similar charges like amortization. For simplicity, Graham simply used the term 'depreciation' across a breadth of items that involve any shrinkage of fixed asset value. The chapter starts by Graham introducing the three problems and considerations of depreciation and similar charges. This also serves as the framework for the following two chapters.

Graham begins with a discussion on whether items should be depreciated based on their purchase price or the new price that items fetches from current market prices. The idea is an intriguing discussion because the later obviously represents the cost of depreciation more accurately, but the application is difficult (not to mention it would lower a company's tax burden).

The rate of depreciation is presented and the different practices used are discussed. Depreciation is such a severe cost to the company that it is found to have a significant influence in the event of a merger, but even more pressing is the event of concealed depreciation. Accounting policies have both been flawed and even omitted to boost earnings in the short run.

The concept of depletion is introduced in the section of amortization charges for the oil and gas industry. An example of depletion is if an oil or gas reserves is gradually being exhausted, as a result, it must be written off against the earnings of the company similar to depreciation. This can be quite complicated for the investor, and Graham suggests various approaches to account for this.

Chapter 34—Outline

A critical analysis of an income statement must pay particular attention to the amounts deducted for depreciation and similar charges. The expenses represent the estimated shrinkage in the value of assets over time.

- Note: Depreciation is referring to the shrinkage of value from a tangible asset such as cars, land, and buildings. Amortization is referring to the shrinkage in value from intangible assets such as patents, leases or capital assets. If a company purchased a car for $10,000, that tangible item would be listed on the company's balance sheet as an asset for $10,000. Assuming that asset (the car) was depreciated over a 5 year period, the company would remove $2,000 of value from that asset (on the balance sheet) and the $2,000 would be listed on the income statement as an expense. This would be for a linear based depreciation method. Therefore, each year, the company's earnings would be $2,000 less until the balance sheet listed the asset for $0.0. It is important to note that the $10,000 purchase is not listed as an expanse on the income statement when the purchase takes place. Instead that expense of that vehicle is spread across the life of the asset. Although depreciation can get quite complex, this basic example is provided to assist readers not familiar with depreciation or amortization expenses and how they arrive onto the income statement and depart the balance sheet.

Leading Questions Relative to Depreciation: If a capital asset has a limited life, provisions must be made to write off the cost of the asset by charges against earnings distributed over the period of the assets life. Although this concept might seem basic, three complications arise.

1. Accounting rules may permit a value other than cost to acquire the asset as the basis for amortization charges.

2. There are numerous ways company can execute their depreciation/amortization charges from the balance sheet to the income statement

3. Sometimes account rules allow companies to make depreciation charges which don't represent the reality of the assets depreciation over time. This makes the analysts job very difficult to assess capital expenditures.

Graham will focus on these problems in this and the next two chapters. First he will look at industrial companies in general, and later special aspects related with oil, mining, and public utility companies.

THE DEPRECIATION BASE

Depreciation Base Other than Cost:

In accounting circles there is support for exercising the depreciation of an asset all at the end of its lifetime, rather than a periodically throughout. If the former was adopted, depreciation charges would vary not only with the value of the identical asset, but also with changes in the character of the item that is expected to replace the one that is worn out.

Graham suggests a variant of the idea: substitute the replacement value of all the fixed assets at a given date, while everything prior is depreciated according to current accounting standards.

An example of a re-evaluation is provided with a write-up on assets prior to the crash in 1929. Graham notes some criticism in accounting circles that are not in-favor or the change. The highlights are listed below:

1. The new values represent existing realities more fairly than the old values.

2. Proper depreciation against these new values are charged in the income statement as an expense—and the company hasn't purchased the new asset yet.

In most cases, companies don't place much interest in ensuring their depreciation charges are representative of their assets' ever-changing replacement costs.

Mark-downs to Reduce Depreciation Charges: A recent markdown of fixed assets has been largely observed. Not in the interests of conservatism, but with the intent of reporting better earnings in the following months so the apparent value of the shares will increase.

Graham believes that excessive write-downs of fixed assets are inexcusable and should not be condoned by the accounting profession. Accountants should refuse to certify a report containing such mark-downs.

Balance Sheet–Income Account Discrepancies: A practice that has been especially prevalent in the case of mining and oil companies, is to mark-up fixed assets and then fail to increase the correspondingly depreciation charges on the income statement. This is done to benefit from the higher valuation in their balance sheet, without accepting the burden of consequently higher depreciation charges against net income.

It should be obvious that no company should use one method of accounting for the balance sheet and another method for the income statement. The way to correct this is to eliminate the mark-up and return to the original cost.

THE RATE OF DEPRECIATION. STANDARD AND NONSTANDARD PRACTICE

1. As Shown by Listing Statements: The vast majority of industrial companies follow the standard policy of charging an appropriate depreciation rate against each class of depreciable assets.

- Note: Different types of assets have different lifetimes to be depreciated against. As a generic example a building might have 20 years, while a car might have 5 years.

2. As Shown by Comparisons of Two Companies: When the analyst knows that a company's depreciation policy differs from the standard, there is special reason to check the adequacy of the allowance. Comparison with a company in the same field may yield significant differences.

Depreciation Charges Often an Issue in Mergers: Comparative depreciation charges can become an issue when two companies plan a merger. As depreciation charges directly influence the income of a company, depreciation methods should also influence the term of consolidation.

Concealed Depreciation: In this section, Graham provides an example of the American Can company to demonstrate that nothing can be taken for granted in security analysis. In 1937, the company had failed to reveal details of its depreciation policy to its shareholders. It was disclosed to stockholders for the first time that the company had been charging sums to operating expenses for "replacements," without providing the amount.

When American Can began to reveal the details of its depreciation policy, it became clear that it had previously understated depreciation, hence overstating the earnings power.

A Case of Excessive Depreciation Charges Concealed by Accounting Methods: Another example of concealed accounting for depreciation was the National Biscuit Company prior to 1922. The company constantly added to the number of its factories, despite the depreciation remaining the same.

According to the financial manuals the company's policy was: "Depreciation is $300,000 per annum, and all items of replacement and building alterations are charged direct to operating expense." Graham notes that sudden doubling in earnings and a rapid increase in net plants would normally also reflect higher depreciation costs. That wasn't the case with this company.

Failure to State Depreciation Charges: Prior to S.E.C. regulations some companies reported earnings after depreciation, but failed to state the amount. Fortunately, this information is now a requirement.

AMORTIZATION CHARGES OF OIL AND MINING COMPANIES

Oil and gas companies are subject to special factors about amortization. In addition to depreciation, they must also allow for depletion of their ore or oil reserves.

In the case of mining, there are development expenses, while oil producers have additional charges for intangible drilling costs and for unproductive leases. These items are important when evaluating the true profits, but accurately accounting for the numerous types of different charges is difficult for the analyst.

Depletion Charges of Mining Companies: Depletion represents the using up of capital assets by turning them into products for sale. It applies to companies producing metals, oil and gas, sulphur, timber, etc. As the holdings, or reserves, of these products are gradually exhausted, their value must gradually be written-off through charges against earnings. This is very similar to inventory in a standard business. Because of the artificial base used in these computations, many companies have omitted the depletion charge from their reports to stockholders.

Independent Calculation by Investor Necessary: In mining, the investor must ordinarily compute his own depletion allowances for his share of the mining property. Using book value cost would be more confusing than helpful. Some companies deduct depletion charges against earnings and others do not.

Depletion and Similar Charges in the Oil Industry: In the oil industry depletion charges are closer related to the actual cost of doing business. Large oil producer normally spends substantial sums of capital each year on new leases and new wells. This is needed to make up for the shrinkage of reserves throughout continued production. In general, depletion charges are cash outlays for the purpose of maintaining reserves and production.

New wells may yield as high as 80% of their total output during the first year. That means that nearly all cost must be written off in a single fiscal period, and most of the "earnings" from this source are in reality a return of the capital thereon. If the investment is not written off rapidly through depletion and other charges, the profit and the value of the property account will both be grossly overstated.

Graham then provides an assessment of how some oil companies would misrepresent the actual lifetime of the asset by extending or shortening the depletion and depreciation of their assets. This was typically exercised so the company could control the market price through earnings manipulation.

The Meaning of These Variations to the Analyst and the Investor.

Graham acknowledges that the differences of accounting methods are highly confusing, and may arouse some resentment in the investor.

Suggested Standards. The analyst should seek to apply a uniform and reasonably conservative rate of amortization that reflects realities of fixed assets. Graham suggests the following standards for depreciation and similar charges, if it is possible to apply them:

1. Depreciation on Tangible Assets. This should always be applied to cost—or to a figure substantially less than cost.

2. Intangible Drilling Costs. Capitalizing these costs, and then writing them off as oil is produced, is the preferable basis for comparative purposes and to supply a fair reflection of current earnings. In comparing companies that use different methods, the analyst must make their best judgment if the company conducts a 100% write-off of depreciation in the first year the asset is owned (assuming the life of the asset is longer than a year).

3. Property Retirement and Abandoned Leases. A loss on property should be charged against the year's earnings, rather than against surplus—like most companies do. For abandoned leases the procedure should be the same.

4. Depletion of Oil Reserves. The proper principle here is that the analyst should allow for depletion based on the current market values of the oil. Unfortunately, tracking this proper valuation for depletion charges is difficult.

Graham finds no satisfactory answer to the dilemma posted in the fourth point. He therefore suggests the following practical compromise to deal with the problem:

1. In the case of integrated oil companies, accept the company's depletion figure as the best available.

2. In the case of companies that are solely or virtually oil producers, the analyst can compute what the market is paying for the total developed oil reserves. This resembles the procedure for mining companies which was explained in an earlier chapter.

OTHER TYPES OF AMORTIZATION OF CAPITAL ASSETS

Leaseholds and Leasehold Improvements: If a lessee is renting a property at a sever discount to the actual cost of owning the property—and the terms of the contract are over a long period of time—there may be significant value to account for.

Oil lands are leased on a standard royalty basis—usually one-eighth of the production. Such leaseholds can be worth much more than the rental payments involved. If a company has paid money for a given leasehold, the cost is regarded as a capital investment that should be written off during the life of the lease. These charges are in reality part of the rent paid for the property, and must therefore be included in current operating expense.

When leased property is improved with assets fixed by the leese, the cost must be written down to nothing during the life of the lease. This is due to the landlord ultimately owning the property and the tethered asset when the lease expires. The annual expense for this purpose is called "amortization of leasehold improvements." Chain-store enterprises frequently invest considerable sums in such leasehold improvements, and consequently the annual write-offs may be of significant importance in their income statements.

Amortization of Patents: In theory, a patent should be dealt with the same way as a mining property; i.e., its cost to the investor should be written off against earnings during its remaining life. The book value of the patent has little relevance for that.

Amortization of Goodwill: This is a matter of very minor importance. A few companies have followed the policy of charging off their goodwill account, against earnings in a number of annual instalments. In modern accounting, Goodwill is continually tested for impairment, but isn't amortized.

Chapter 35—Summary

Public Utility Depreciation Policies

In the beginning of this chapter Graham explains the differences between depreciation theory and practice with the public utility sector. He finds that too many companies have intentionally used misleading accounting practices to misstate depreciation, hence the earnings of the company.

Seven depreciation policies are presented and divided into two categories. The retirement reserve method is especially criticized.

Graham initiates a discussion of whether the analyst should use the reported depreciation or a variant derived from an assessment of the company's charged income tax. Graham comes forward with 5 compelling arguments why depreciation based on the income tax figure is the preferred choice. In the end, Graham makes observations based on depreciation polices and the market prices of those corresponding stocks.

Chapter 35—Outline

Omission of Depreciation Charges. Public utilities is a field where a proper depreciation is important to include; still history has shown a vast discrepancy between theory and practice. Depreciation is not just for bookkeeping purposes, but instead it is a true representation of an actual decrease in capital value.

Over time depreciation charges are eventually found to be equivalent to actual cash outlays. They are just as much a business expense as wages or rents.

Other Misleading Practices. A fairly prevalent practice is the deduction of only part of the depreciation charge from earnings. This balance was taken out of the surplus account, thereby misstating earnings for the current year. This practice unbalances the books and eventually displays a windfall of expenses once the surplus account is depleted.

An illustration of Tricky Accounting. One company had chosen a practice with very low depreciation. After three years, the company made a formal confession of their misstep. However, the cure was handled in a very unorthodox manner.

Inadequate Depreciation Revealed by Transfer from Surplus and Reserves. Graham shows an example with a company called Brooklyn Union Gas to illustrate the impact on the income statement when amortization is not properly deducted. He shows how overstatement of earnings can be revealed by the huge transfers from surplus and contingency reserves.

A Variety of Depreciation Policies. In this section, Graham provides seven different depreciation policies.

A. Depreciation Proper.

1. *Straight-line Method.* Each class of depreciable property is written down by equal annual charges during the period of its estimated life.

2. *Sinking-fund Method.* The effect of this method is to make the deductions somewhat smaller in the earlier years and correspondingly higher in the later years. This is because depreciation is assumed to earn interest until the property is retired

3. *The Over-all Method.* Here a single annual percentage to the entire depreciable property account is used, instead of varying rates to different classes of assets. The object is to arrive at a simple approximation of the actual depreciation.

B. Retirement Reserve Methods.

The intention of a retirement reserve is to have funds available when and as an asset retires. Over any long period of time, proper depreciation and proper retirement allowances should yield the same results. In reality the majority of retirement reserve policies operate simply to understate the current loss of property value and thus to overstate the earnings.

Various methods of calculating retirement reserves are:

4. *Percentage of Gross.* This method would tend to approximate a regular depreciation rate if the percentage taken were adequate. Generally this is not the case. In one example Graham shows an 8% deductions of gross, but tax deductions of 30%.

5. *Fixed Rate per Unit of Product.* This method resembles the previous and is subject to the same criticism. Instead of a percentage of gross product, an example used is $2.7 in depreciation for every thousand kilowatt hours sold.

6. *Over-all Percentage of Gross for Maintenance and Depreciation Combined.* By this method the larger the amount spent for maintenance the smaller the amount saved in a reserve for depreciation.

7. *Discretionary Deductions.* The annual deduction is largely based on the judgment of the management. It might be the same or varying amount from year to year.

Double Accounting Policies on Depreciation. Regardless of what method is followed in the annual reports, practically every company follows the straight-line basis of depreciation in computing its income tax. This imposes a problem to the investor. The investor must determine whether the depreciation is representative of the linear or non-linear erosion that takes place on the value of the asset over time.

Reasons for Accepting, in General, the Income Tax Base. Graham presents five major reasons for accepting the income tax figure rather than the income statement as basis of depreciation:

1. The straight-line basis follows a definite and logical accounting theory. If there is an excessive deduction, the Treasury Department won't accept it.

2. The inadequacy of the "retirement reserve" idea in general, has been shown by the necessity in many cases of making large transfers from surplus to support the retirement reserve.

3. Since 1934 there has been an almost universal increase in the retirement allowances. This can be perceived as a strong indicator that past allowances were too small and therefore an overstatement of earnings.

4. A number of state commissions and the Federal commissions have now ordered companies within their jurisdictions to follow the income tax depreciation base.

5. As previously found, when giving a real alternative, the investor in fixed-value securities must invariably apply the more stringent test of soundness.

Instance When Income Tax Basis Should Be Rejected or Questioned. While Graham in general believes in accepting income tax basis, there may be times when figures in the annual report should be accepted, or even to seek a third basis. Although a few specific examples are given, Graham acknowledges the difficulty in providing specific guidelines, as the stock investor needs to know the company really well.

Practical Effect of Varying Depreciation Policies. While the reader might not think the subject of utility depreciation policy interesting, it has a bearing of the greatest practical importance on the market behavior of the stocks. As an example companies that charged inadequate depreciation prior to 1934 were generally overvalued in the stock market, because investors gave inadequate attention to their overstated earnings.

Chapter 36—Summary

Amortization charges from the investor's viewpoint

Graham starts out with a hypothetical example of three companies all engaged in the trucking business. This example shows how the depreciation, based on the book value of a fixed asset, distorts the earnings. For the stock investor, this example shows why it is important to understand concepts like depreciation, amortization, and write-downs, when valuing a stock The reader can quickly see how the maket is often focused on earnings and not the numbers behind. Graham continually returns to this example to prove his points.

 Next, Graham explains the concept of *expended depreciation.* This number can be seen as the maintenance cost of running the business. Simply trusting the numbers that the company reports isn't recommended. Instead, Graham discusses the importance of the investors to think independently and make his own estimates. He acknowledges that in practice one needs to really know the business before this type of assessment may be possible.

Several examples are provided that show how earnings can be manipulated by a write-down or a write-off, and subsequent low depreciation charges. Graham found that while it was earlier the practice to write fixed assets up to inflate share prices, it is now more common to do the opposite, however the intention stayed the same—management's attempt to manipulate the trading price.

Patents are also examined. Here the difference between the book value of a fixed asset and the true value of an asset is emphasized. Another method for accounting for this intangible depreciation (or amortization) is introduced to the reader. Again, it is argued that one's estimates for a single or bulk group of patents, is prone to miscalculations.

Chapter 36—Outline

Several references are made to depreciation and depletion that may technically be valid from an accounting point, but often fail to reflect the current situation for the stock buyer.

Problem Indicated by Hypothetical Example. To prove his point Graham sets up a simplified hypothetical example.

Companies A, B, and C are all engaged in the trucking business. Each has a single truck; each possess a 100 shares of stock, no par, and each earns $2,000 per annum before depreciation.

Company A paid $10,000 for its truck.

Company B paid $5,000 for its truck.

Company C paid $5,000 for its truck but followed "an ultra-conservative policy" and wrote its value down to $1 immediately after it was purchased.

It is further assumed that Company A's truck was purchased for too expensive of a price. The capability of each truck is therefore the same, so the three companies can be perceived identically. Given a 4 year life time the income statement will read:

Item	Company A	Company B	Company C
EBITDA	$2,000	$2,000	$2,000
Depreciation (25%)	$2,500	$1,250	$ 0
EBIT	-$ 500	$ 750	$2,000
Earnings per Share	$ 0	$ 7.5	$ 20

Typical Market Appraisals.

The absurdity of these valuations should be clear. A company with a less valuable asset in terms of accounting is worth considerable more than the company with a higher value asset. This is done by the single gesture of writing down company C's assets to almost nothing immediately upon the purchase.

A More Rational Approach. The question is now how an investor would value the businesses. A more practical approach would be to include the fair value of the respective assets and add that to the cash holdings. The investor might consider which depreciation method that should be used.

Practical application of foregoing Reasoning. Graham shows another example of a company that appears to not make money when looking at the earnings, but is somehow generating a large amount of cash. When comparing what is spent on the company's plant and spares with the depreciation charges, one finds the explanation: depreciation is not a cash outlay, but deducted as an expense on the income statement. As a result, the company is reporting no income, yet the cash account continues to grow because displayed income is being off-set by depreciation charges.

How to Determine the Proper Depreciation Charge. The investor or the analyst must come up with an estimate for depreciation which aligns with the actual conditions of the business. In reality, exact knowledge about the depreciation is impossible. Graham suggests the analyst formulate some rough estimates based on the discoverable facts. While he realize that this would not be accurate either, the upside is that it would be closer to reality than the companies reported figures in irregular situations.

Concept of Expended Depreciation. The primary reason for reducing a company's depreciation charges is because it doesn't properly reflect the company's cash flow. In short, as an asset's life continues to get older, the value that it is listed for on the company's balance sheet will continue to decrease. As a result, an investor should see the value of tangible and intangible assets slowly decrease in value over time. Although this might be true for an individual asset, the total value for all assets may not depict this from a cursory look. The reason why is due to the replenishment of those assets once they are retired. For example, if a company owns 5 cars and each car was purchased 1 year apart from each other, the change in book value will not likely change. The balance sheet would generally show no change in value for these five years (in aggregate) because as each car's value expires, it's being replaced on the balance sheet by the value of the new car.

Long-term Depreciation a Form of Obsolescence. Graham then discusses which amount that should be taken as a reserve for wearing out the entire PP&E. Most theoretical discussions resemble that of a truck where the asset is completely replaced after a predefined number of years with respect to its useful like. For instance a plant may not be wearing out, but rather being obsolete due to changes in the industry and the status of the corporation. This risk is rather due to the investment and not accounting, hence it should be incorporated in the price and not in the depreciation, as it is a business risk. Therefore the carrying value of the asset should be adjusted accordingly. This value test for asset impairment should be conducted quarterly by the company's management.

Application of Foregoing in Determining Earning Power. Companies that are similar to a railroad should be perceived differently in terms of depreciation. The lifetime appears to be indefinite, but needs maintenance, renewals and repair to a large degree. Here, only the expended depreciation should be deducted from earnings, which was explained earlier.

Problems of evaluating Earning Power. Again Graham discusses how difficult it is to evaluate earnings power dependent on the knowledge of depreciation. He again stresses that the investor may use a depreciation allowance different from the company to assess it's value properly.

Depreciation on Apartment and Office Buildings. Both depreciation on real estate and the depreciation of bonds are discussed here. For the psychical asset it is again a question of the building being obsolete, and not worn out. For bonds purchased at a large discount to face value, the investor's write-off and depreciation would be based on a cost much lower to him, than the book value that is subject to conventional depreciation. In short, the asset can't be depreciated for more than the price that was paid to acquire it.

Inadequate Allowance for Depreciation. This is an important section and Graham's main point: assets should not be written down in large amounts early in the assets life simply to make the earnings-power appear more abundant during the assets final years of life. This misrepresents the true cash flow of the business and is nothing more than a tactic to deceive the public. An example is shown again that proves a significant write-off will decrease the depreciation charges for the years to come.

Earnings Manufactured from Depreciation Account. Again the reader's attention is redirected to company C in the example of trucks. Depreciation must be allowed, it cannot be eliminated by book keeping entries. A company doesn't make more money simply because the asset is effectively not listed. Instead, the company's earnings will appear to come in spurts and look unpredictable over-time.

Other Examples of Elimination of Fixed Assets: Here other examples of companies that have been writing down fixed assets to as little as $1 is introduced. For these companies subsequent charges for depreciation were reduced to less than a suitable figure.

Stock Watering Reversed. This manipulation of asset value by writing the book value up and down is interrelated with the value of the stock. Earlier a practice where stocks were written up far above the actual cost, which was known as *stock watering* was used. This process was heavily criticized, as this would inflate the stock prices by the higher book value of the fixed assets.

This practice has now reversed, since so many investors only pay attention to the earnings and not the book value. Graham repeats the poor Wall Street practice of writing-down a large portion of an asset early in it's life in order to prop-up earnings in the "out-years". The idea that such sleight-of-hand could actually add to the value of a security is nothing short of preposterous.

Purchaser's Amortization of Ore Reserves. The difference in allowances for amortization between the investor and the company is most clear during depletion of ore reserves. While the amounts charged off by a mining company for depletion are based upon certain technical considerations, it is likely quite irrelevant to the stockholders' situation.

The Purchaser's Amortization Calculation. In the situation where the mining company does not charge for deletion in the annual report a general approach can be made. Where the life of a mining property is limited, the investor's own calculation of amortization should be deducted from earnings. He can base this on three factors. 1) The price paid for the mining property. 2) The earnings before depreciation and depletion. 3) The minimum life of the mine, and alternatively, the probability of life.

Purchasers Amortization of Oil Reserves. Graham applies the principles above by using an oil producer as an example. He emphasized that the depreciation and depletion charges per barrel are found by dividing the estimated remaining oil reserves into the net value of the properties on the books.

Purchaser's Amortization of Patents. A large number of important manufacturing companies' own patents that are carried on their books at $1 or at their cost price, which most often is a small amount. It is standard accounting practice to write off such cost by equal annual charges to earnings during the life of the patent, which is 17 years from the date it is granted.

- Note: Today the rule for amortization is different. In brief, it is dependent on the shortest time for either the useful life, or the time that the company owns the right to the patent.

The investor's viewpoint requires an entirely different approach. The question for him is how much he is paying for the patent, when he buys the stock at a given price. This is the amount he must use for writing-off subsequent earnings.

General rule. In reality no single calculation shown above will represent stocks wholistically. For big companies it is even harder since they have a bulk of patents and intangible items.

Examples. Graham looks at two companies that had significant increases and decreases in earnings after a patent expired, he concludes that patents should not be valued by quantitative factors.

Special cases. In some special cases when a company's business primarily consists of collecting royalties on a patent or a group of patents, some finite provisions can be made. This provision must be related to the price the investor paid for his interest in the patent, and not on the book value of the patent. Graham shows three examples to prove his point.

Chapter 37—Summary

Significance of The Earnings Record

When conducting security analysis of the income statement Graham points out two particular items. The first is to arrive at normalized earnings for the present year. The second is to use past earnings records to explain the future. Graham strongly suggests that the analyst should make qualitative analysis along-side their quantitative work.

Graham also examines how the analyst should look at the trend of earnings compared to the average. In his opinion the stock market is putting too much emphasis on the trend. That said, he repeats his position that a valuation cannot be based solely on the current earnings.

He provides words of caution to the analysts that think a company can continue to grow and prosper at uncharacteristic levels forever. On the other hand a decline in earnings must likewise be analyzed from a qualitative point of view. The analysis of earnings should be a qualitative assessment as much as a numbers assessment.

Chapter 37—Outline

By examining the income statement critically, one can arrive at a fair and informed overview for the period studied. This is only part of the security analysis assessment. Another part, which is both harder and more important, is examining if the past can explain the future. Graham finds the latter part less satisfactory because laborious studies often lead to unreliable and valueless outcomes. With that said, the past does provide clues into a company's stability and potentially its general direction.

The Concept of Earning Power: This concept, which is basically the average earnings per share, should be seen over a number of years. One should notice if the observed years are all surrounded by the average. This is preferred to very volatile earnings, as repeated occurrences are more impressive than a single occurrence.

Quantitative Analysis Should Be Supplemented by Qualitative Considerations: Graham brings forward an excellent point that the investor needs to be aware of when studying earnings:

> *Quantitative data is useful only to the extent that's supported by a qualitative survey of the enterprise.*

To illustrate his example a steel company is used. While current and past earnings are one thing, Graham aims to calculate 'normal earnings'. He suggests that the national output of steel and the market position should be considered as a part of a qualitative analysis. Reported earnings cannot be viewed without relative factors.

Current Earnings Should Not Be the Primary Basis of Appraisal: Current earnings governs the market price of common stock prices more than the long term average. While a private business might earn twice as much as their average years, their local market price would never be purchased based on the extraordinary year of earnings. With Wall Street, it operates differently. The market price typically corresponds very closely too the earnings regardless of the abnormalities in earnings. This is an important difference between Wall Street and ordinary businesses. As the speculative public shares vision with Wall Street it would seem logical to buy cheap stock at temporarily suppressed earnings and sell them at inflated levels created by the opposite effect.

The Classical Formula for "Beating the Stock Market. While this is an accepted strategy for beating the stock market it is not that simple. For one thing, the timing of the market is hard, and the underlying values of the stocks continuously change.

On Wall Street, the common assumption is that trends are likely to continue or persist regardless of qualitative circumstances. Experience shows that such developments do not often occur. While the analyst, on occasion, can place predominant weight on the recent earnings, rather than the average, persuasive evidence has to be present.

Average vs. Trend of Earnings: Wall Street places great emphasis on the trends of earnings. As shown in this example there is a fundamental difference between the average and the trend.

Company	Earned per share in successive years						7th (current)	Average	Trend
	1	2	3	4	5	6			
A	$1	$2	$3	$4	$5	$6	$7	$4	Excellent
B	$7	$7	$7	$7	$7	$7	$7	$7	Neutral
C	$13	$12	$11	$10	$9	$8	$7	$6	Bad

While the trend of company A should definitely be taken into account, it is not the same as if the trend will continue into the future. On the contrary one must consider why this might not happen. Competition, regulation, law of diminishing returns is all something that speaks against a continued growth. Instead of taking the continued trend for granted, the analyst must approach

Company A with caution and seek a reasonable margin of safety. Company's like this, often fetch a very large premium.

Attitude of Analyst Where Trends are Upward. If a qualitative study of company A is positive, which it often should be, the analyst should base future results on a conservative estimate of what the company can currently produce. If the current business conditions are not unusually good, the earning power might be set at $7 and perhaps the investment value of $140 dependent on the analyst's approach and capitalization rate (a price of $140 would be a 20X earnings multiple).

Attitude of Analyst Where Trend Is Downward: For company C the analyst must assign great weight to the unfavorable trend and the reasons why. However one can't make hasty conclusions that this trend will persist either. Again, a qualitative study of the company must be made. This is just similar to a sensible businessman looking into the pros and cons of a privately owned enterprise. Graham shows the example of a company that lost only a little earnings in a recession where competitors would suffer more severely. Here the earning power should be focused on the average rather than the trend.

Deficits a Qualitative, Not a Quantitative Factor: When a company reports a deficit for the year, it is customary to calculate the amount in dollars per share or in relation to interest requirements. This is not a valid approach. Instead the attention of the analyst should be directed elsewhere.

When an average is taken over a period that includes a number of deficits, some questions must arise as to whether or not the resultant figure is really indicative of the earning power. This is especially true if the company has volatile numbers. Another consideration is if the 10 year period uses extraordinary figures—if so, they should be relatively discounted across all picks. The Great Depression in the 1930's could be an example.

Intuition Not a Part of the Analyst's Stock in Trade: Unless there is a reason to think otherwise, the past record is accepted as a basis for judging the future.

Only sound reasoning should be made by the analyst. It would be unreasonable to expect an enormous increase in cigarette consumption since 1915 (during Graham's writing) or the decline in the cigar business.

Analysis of the Future Should Be Penetrating Rather than Prophetic. In short, the investor should not be reliant on the company's performance to improve in order to justify a premium price. Instead, the future results should be penetrating, with respect to the current capacity to earn and the price the market is trading the stock for. Graham provides an example of a company to demonstrate his opinion.

Large Profits Frequently Transitory: Many analysts find reasons to say a company will continue to have indefinite prosperity from past trend results. An example, are gadgets that are normally short lived. The market price of such a stock should not be bearing the usual ratio to current and average earnings.

A similar consideration could be made for a certain attractive industry. When capital flows into new industries it may result in overcapacity and keen competition—dragging profits down for individual company's in the long-haul.

Chapter 38—Summary

Specific Reasons for Questioning or Rejecting The Past Record

This chapter provides additional arguments for questioning the past record of earnings. In every situation a qualitative assessment of future earnings must be made, and Graham discussed how deceptive non-recurring earnings are to earning power. This applies to both revenues and costs.

Through detailed analysis, a vast discrepancy between the value and the price of a stock can be discovered. Solely looking at previous and past earnings to determine the future is not prescribed, instead, a balanced and holistic determination is paramount to a an analysts success.

Chapter 38—Outline

When analyzing an individual company, each of the governing elements in the operating results must be studied for signs of unfavorable changes. Governing elements may vary, but if the analyst was assessing the general factors of a mining company, they might focus on areas like: (1) life of the mine, (2) annual output, (3) production costs and (4) selling price.

Rate of Output and Operating Costs

Already having examined the first point (1) in earlier chapters, Graham continues examining point two (2) and point three (3) by analyzing a mining company and the sources of its profits. His analysis shows that only a limited portion of the profits in the future would come from the lower cost properties. If the future earnings had to be supported by higher cost, it would make the current facts speculative and much riskier.

Freeport Sulphur Company. A similar example is found with Freeport Sulphur Company. This company had a large part of their earnings from one piece of property for several years and then it became non-operational. As a result, there are no guarantees for similar results in the future. The learning point is that a high valuation based on future prospects is highly speculative. Graham points out that when the stock market moves away from sound sense and business experience, the common stock buyer will inevitable lose money.

The Future Price of the Product: Looking at the fourth (4) element (selling price) the analyst can intelligently say very little about future prices, except that they fall outside the realm of sound prediction. Any prediction outside of that might be plausible from time to time, but must be justified by facts.

Change in Status of Low-cost Producers: When analyzing the individual company one must also look at the overall cost level, and in which direction it can be expected to change. The cost price will be a determinant for the selling price.

Anomalous Prices and Price Relationships in the History of the I.R.T. System: One example where the price of the stock was far away from the value is visible when looking at Interborough Rapid Transit System in New York City. Looking at the past and current earnings, the company looked to have a prosperous future, but a closer analysis revealed a different picture. New transit facilities were being constructed, and under a strict contract governed by New York City. The contract was capping the potential income, and the earning power of the company would therefore severely decline in the near future. Even under favorable conditions, it would take more than 30 years before any income could be distributed with the company.

The analysis not only showed that the current selling price was far above the value of the stock. It also showed that when there is an upper limit of earnings or value being fixed, there is usually a danger that the actual figure could be less.

What happened afterwards for Interborough Rapid Transit System was that earnings indeed were non-recurrent and temporary. As earning power declined it ran quickly into severe financial problems.

Chapter 39—Summary

Price-Earnings Ratios for Common Stocks. Adjustments for Changes in Capitalization

This chapter discusses price earnings as a valuation technique. Graham suggests that a multiple based on earnings is not plausible, and a general rule or formula for valuation by definition is illogical. He also stresses that stock prices are not carefully computed, but are a result of human reactions. In continuation of this theme, Graham gives us his famous quote: *The stock market is a voting machine rather than a weighing machine.* In this chapter, the time dimension of this quote is not included (voting machine in the short run, and weighing machine in the long run), but there is no doubt that this concept can be read between the lines throughout the chapter.

Under "favorable conditions for high-quality companies," Graham suggests an upper limit of 20 times average earnings for the past 5-10 years. Ordinarily, a business can be bought for 12-12.5 times average earnings—but while price is a necessary condition for the sound investor, price alone is not sufficient. Financial setup, favorable business conditions, and proper management are conditions that also need to be met. A good conservative investment leaves an upside for the satisfactory prospect. The opposite is not the case.

Three categories of business are examined. One category is speculative due to high prices; the next category is speculative due to instable earnings; while the last category is a good investment because it passes the quantitative tests: stable earnings, reasonable average earnings to market price, conservative financial setup, and a strong working capital.

Finally, allowances for changes in capitalization and participating interests are examined, in order to provide a comprehensive overview and ensure that the investor's earnings calculations are not distorted.

Chapter 39—Outline

Prior to the bull market of 1927-1929, a price of 10 times earnings was the accepted standard for measuring common stock. The exact multiplier depended on the nature and earnings records of the business.

- Note: This is a discussion of the general investment rule that if earnings for a share are $1, the stock price should be around $10.

Beginning about 1927, the standard started to change. Perceived good stocks were traded at a higher multiple, and favored groups of stocks like public utilities and chain stores were traded even higher. This was justified by the assumption that the upward trends seen for longer and shorter periods in the past would continue.

After 1932, the tendency was for higher prices-to-earnings multiples, due to the sharp drop in long-term interest rates.

Exact Appraisal Impossible: A security analysis cannot provide a general rule for proper valuation. Practically speaking, there is no such thing. Also, the idea of basing the valuation on current earnings is absurd since earnings are constantly changing. Stock market prices are not carefully computed, but are the result of human reactions. The stock market is a voting machine rather than a weighing machine.

Limited Functions of the Analyst in the Field Stock Price Appraisal: Graham repeats that, as facts and human behavior change, the security analyst must not follow a general rule for his valuations. However, Graham proposes some limited functions:

1. He may set-up a basis for conservative or investment valuation of common stocks, as distinguished from speculative valuations.

2. He may point out the significance of: (a) the capitalization structure; and (b) the source of income, as bearing upon the valuation of a given stock issue.

3. He may find unusual elements in the balance sheet which affect the implications of the earnings picture.

A Suggested Basis of Maximum Appraisal for Investment: Both the investor and the speculator in common stocks are dependent on future rather than past earnings. They should be conservative in their estimates, ensuring that they are proven by actual performance over a period of time.

The profits of the most recent year might be accepted as an indicator of future earnings, if (1) general business conditions in that year were not exceptionally good, (2) the company has shown an upward trend of earnings for some years past and (3) the investor's study of the industry leaves him confident about its continued growth.

In most instances, the investor will look at the average earnings in the past 5-10 years. The investor could allow for a more liberal valuation if current earnings are above average or the company has better-than-average prospects. It is suggested that the upper limit for a common stock valuation should not exceed 20 times average earnings. Though this rule might seem arbitrary, it is not entirely so, as we must remember to leave room for a margin of safety.

Note: A P/E of 20 equates to a 5% return – assuming earnings remain constant and are treated as free cash flow to the shareholder.

Higher Prices May Prevail for Speculative Commitments: It is not implied that it is a mistake to pay more than 20 times average earnings. What is suggested is that this is speculative, which does not exclude the possibility of being highly profitable. It should be noted that few people are consistently fortunate in their speculative operations.

Other Requisites for Common Stocks of Investment Grade and a Corollary Thereof: As 20 times average earnings is the upper limit, the purchase price for ordinary businesses should be substantially less. 12 or 12.5 times average earnings can be suggested as a necessary multiplier but not a sufficient condition. It must be emphasized that many other factors must be present, including the financial setup, not-unsatisfactory prospects, and proper management. Next, Graham provides us with an interesting point: <u>An attractive common-stock investment is an attractive speculation.</u> This is true because, if a common stock can meet the demand of a conservative investor, then he gets full value for his money, plus satisfactory future prospects. Logical reasoning would conclude that the common stock also has a fair chance of appreciating in market value.

Examples of Speculative and Investment Common Stocks. Graham is not fond of Wall Street making lists of attractive common stocks. He lists three categories to illustrate his point. (A) These stocks are sold at a multiple considerably more than 20 times average earnings, and become speculative solely based on price. In other words, they all require large future growth to justify the price. (B) Other stocks are speculative not because of the average earnings, but the speculative element of the instability of earnings. (C) This is the group that passes the quantitative tests of investment quality. These tests include the following:

1. Earnings have been reasonably stable

2. Average earnings have a satisfactory ratio to market price

3. Financial setup is sufficiently conservative, and the working capital position is strong

ALLOWANCES FOR CHANGES IN CAPITALIZATION

When dealing with past records of earnings on a per-share basis, the analyst must adjust to changes in capitalization. This might be confusing if the capitalization is not adjusted for stock splits and stock dividend. The number of shares outstanding might also change due to conversion of various securities like bonds and preferred stocks.

ALLOWANCES FOR PARTICIPATING INTERESTS

When calculating earnings for the common shareholder, the participating interests must also be included. (As the reader might recall from previous chapters, participating interests is a new structure of dividing income when it increases.) It does not matter if the money has not been paid out yet. Similar allowances must be made for the effect of management contracts.

General Rule

The intrinsic value of a common stock preceded by convertible securities cannot reasonably be appraised at a higher figure than would be justified if all convertible securities were exercised in full. The same is the case if it is subject to dilution through the exercise of stock options, or through participating privileges enjoyed by other senior security.

Chapter 40—Summary

Capitalization Structure

In this chapter, Graham examines whether a company's capital structure (division of funding between stocks and bonds) has any influence on the company's total value. He starts by comparing three hypothetical, identical companies only differentiated by their capital structure.

Following a careful analysis, Graham concludes the following: The optimum capitalization structure for any enterprise includes senior securities to the extent that they may be safely issued and bought for investment. The practical implication of this is that, under safe circumstances, no debt leads to an inefficient use of the shareholder's capital. On the other hand, too much debt leaves no room for an appropriate margin of safety, as the interest coverage ratio is very small and risky.

In theory and practice, companies that are overcapitalized can trade higher and lower than their value, dependent on the state of the market. During "good times", for instance, an overcapitalized stock is often traded above the value and vice versa. Graham raises the question of whether the investor could benefit from speculative behavior. While not providing a direct answer, he lists the circumstances where it might be possible, but at the same time warns about the dilemma any speculator ultimately faces: he can only hold for further gain using the profit he has already accrued.

Chapter 40—Outline

Companies with identical earnings power appear to be valuated differently solely due to their capitalization based on common stocks and/or bonds. Graham introduces the following example:

Company	Earnings for common stock	Value of common stock	Value of bonds	Total value of company
A	$ 1,000,000	$ 12,000,000	$ —	$ 12,000,000
B	$ 760,000	$ 9,000,000	$ 6,000,000	$ 15,000,000
C	$ 520,000	$ 6,000,000	$ 12,000,000	$ 18,000,000

All three companies have $1,000,000 in earning power and are identical, apart from their capital structures. Company B and company C have issues $6,000,000 and $12,000,000 in bonds, respectively, at 4%. This is also the reason company B only has earnings for common stock on $760,000 (1,000,000-4%*6,000,000).

It is also assumed that the value of the common stock is 12 times earnings. Graham then raises the question: "Does this mean that the fair value of an enterprise can be arbitrarily increased or decreased by changing the relative proportions of senior securities and common stock?"

Can the Value of an Enterprise Be Altered through Arbitrage Variations in Capital Structure? To answer this question, Graham once more examines companies A and B. The bonds for company B are assumed to be sold at around 100 since the interest can be paid four times (1,000,000 / 6,000,000*4% = 4.17). Another realistic assumption is that both companies' shares can be sold at 12 times earnings. While it can be argued that company A's shares must be deemed more valuable since there is no debt and the risk is somewhat smaller, it is equally true that company B's shares are more responsive to an increase in earnings, as seen in the table below.

Assumed earnings	Earned per share		Change in earnings per share from base	
	Company A	Company B	Company A	Company B
$1,000,000	$10	$7.60	(Base)	(Base)
$ 750,000	$7.5	$5.10	-25%	-33%
$1,250,000	$12.5	$10.10	+25%	+33%

Based on the figures, we are led back to the original conclusion that company B must be worth $3,000,000 or 25% more than company A. This is a difference solely created by the capital structure.

Principle of Optimum Capitalization Structure: Though this valuation seems illogical, it can actually be supported by the behavior of the stock market.

The common-stock buyer would rarely recognize the bond element in the common stock, and even if he did, he would be unwilling to pay extra for that. This leads us to an important principle: The optimum capitalization structure for any enterprise includes senior securities to the extent that they may safely be issued and bought for investment.

This safe environment may be composed both of a working capital of no less than the bond value (for company B that would be $6,000,000), and other conditions, as presented in Chapter 13. Under such circumstances, a very conservative capitalization based only on the shareholders' equity would make the shareholders' dollars less productive.

Corporate Practices Resulting in Shortage of Sound Industrial Bonds: Investors generally prefer strongly funded corporation-issued bonds, as these offer a wider range of choices and make the sale of unsound bonds less likely.

Appraisal of Earnings Where Capital Structure is Top-Heavy: In order to take the discussion of capital structure a step further, Graham also examines company C. The value was calculated to be as much as $18,000,000, given the assumption that bonds could be sold at par, and stocks at 12 times earnings.

The assumption of the sales price of the bond is clearly wrong as the interest payment would only be covered two times (1,000,000 / 12,000,000*4% = 2.08). In other words, the bonds are risky and therefore wouldn't fetch their par value. Bond owners in this case would be willing to accept only a 4% return, while shareholders would get an 8% return, all voting power and half of the earnings.

This example also shows the impact of the interest rate. Assume that we also had a company D with $12,000,000 in bonds, just like company C, but carrying a 6% interest rate. The interest coverage would be very small (1,000,000 / 12,000,000*6% = 1.39). Imagine an investor who would accept the 4% bond from company C because the coverage ratio was two, while not accepting the 6% bond from company D because the ratio was smaller. Such discrimination is not intelligent. The main takeaway from this is that a margin of safety principle must be applied. A safety margin should not appear by a mere lowering of the interest rate. The same reasoning would apply to dividends and preferred stocks.

Since company C's bonds are unsafe, they can be expected to be sold at a vast discount to par. The exact price is hard to estimate, but it might be that the entire value of the company would be valued at less than $15,000,000 (company B) or even $12,000,000 (company A). Also, the presence of these bonds might cause investors to pay less than 12 times earnings. In rare cases, a higher market valuation than $18,000,000 could be possible; however, such a situation would be unsound and pose extra risk to the investor.

The Factor of Leverage is Speculative Capitalization Structure: For the speculator, the common stock has a built-in advantage. Consider again company C and an increase of 25% in earnings. Earnings per share of a common stock would increase about 50% ($5.2 to $7.7). Because of this, speculative capitalized enterprises can be sold at somewhat high prices during good markets. On the contrary, the same venture might be undervalued during a depression.

The real advantage, however, lies in the fact that the stock can advance more than it can decline. An example is provided, from 1921 to 1929. While the stock price increased 400-fold, gross earnings increased only 2.6 times. While stocks around 1929 were sold at very high multiples, the capital structure provides us with an additional explanation. By issuing mainly senior securities, the balance per share grew 14-fold during that time.

Speculative Capitalization May Cause Valuation of Total Enterprise at an Unduly Low Figure: A practical example of company C would be A.E. Staley Company. In the Depression of 1933, it was highly capitalized, resulting in an over-deflated low share price. These situations leave room for very high appreciation of the market price, because earnings can rapidly increase when business conditions improve. This company was an example of this as the share price appreciated 10 times in only 6 years.

Speculative Attractiveness of "Shoestring" Common Stocks Considered: Based on the A.E Stanley Company, it is easy to conclude that the investor can wait and exploit abnormal and temporary conditions. While this would not be an *investment*, it may be seen as intelligent or even scientific *speculation*.

Practical Aspects of the Foregoing: When putting this into practice, the purchaser of speculatively capitalized common stocks must be considered under general or market conditions. There must also be diversification and sound judgment in selecting the right companies.

Senior capital for the company should be held in preferred shares rather than in bonds, as this would limit the risk of bankruptcy during bad times, permitting the common stockholder to wait for better times (preferred shares can omit dividend payments, while bonds in general are obliged to pay out coupon payments).

We must not, however, forget that as soon as the investor sees his security increase in price, he is in a dilemma. He can only hold for further gain with the profit he has already accrued.

Chapter 41—Summary

Low-Priced Common Stocks.
Analysis of The Source of Income

LOW-PRICED STOCKS

In this chapter, Graham speaks about low-priced stocks and why they are popular in the speculative public. Studies show that while low-priced stocks offer great opportunity for speculation, they also demonstrate that buyers typically lose money because they buy for the wrong reasons.

This chapter continues where Graham left us in the preceding chapter. Here, he continues with the speculative capital structure, but now he compares this situation to a company that has high production costs. In this situation, an increase in sales price or profit would be multiplied, percentage-wise, to the company with no speculative capital structure or lower costs.

Sources of income are also introduced in this chapter. Three companies are presented, with the common denominator being that the sources of income do not originate from the nature of the businesses, but from other income sources like bonds, rentals, and leases. The advice from Graham is for the investor to examine the sources of income before investing, and for owners to insist on solving illogical arrangements.

Chapter 41—Outline

The majority of speculative capitalized companies described in the preceding chapter are typically "low-priced." Clearly the definition of something being low-priced is arbitrary. Stock prices below $10 fall into that category without question; stocks above $20 would be excluded, so logically the dividing line must be somewhere in between.

Arithmetical Advantage of Low-priced Issues: Low-priced stocks offer the advantage of being more likely to appreciate than decline. Securities are found to rise more readily from 10 to 40 than from 100 to 400, and because of this, the speculative public would rather buy into stocks of lower numerical value.

Graham cites a study that confirms his thesis that low-price stocks tend to fluctuate more. The study also found that in bull markets, low-priced stock increased more compared to higher-priced stocks, and that these would not lose their superior value in a recession.

The study also concludes that low-priced stocks offer great opportunity for speculation, even if companies are similar, with only the numerical stock price as a difference.

- Note: In theory, the stock price should not tell you anything about the business. A business with 1,000 shares at $100 has exactly the same market price as a business with 10,000 shares at $10. Graham's comments and thesis are based on the psychology of the individuals involved in the market.

Some of the Reasons Most Buyers of Low-priced Issues Lose Money: It would seem logical for a buyer to prefer lower-priced stocks. However, this is not always the best route, since the buyer may well lose money. The reason for this is the public buys issues that are sold to them; hence the sales effort focuses on benefiting the seller, not the buyer. As a consequence, the public may be buying lowed-priced stocks for the wrong reasons. One such reason could be bad financial conditions; another could be simply issuing a very high number of shares, which combined are priced higher than the actual value.

Observation of the stock market reveals that companies that are due to face receivership due to bad earnings are likely to be traded at higher volumes. The reason for this behavior is the insiders' desire to dispose of their assets, sometimes resulting in rigorous efforts to persuade the unwary public to buy them. On the other hand, one could look at low-priced stocks fulfilling the conditions of speculative attractiveness, as shown in Chapter 40. In this case, there is no pressure to sell, hence no effort to create buying, and no attention in the media. This analysis may explain why the public almost always buys the wrong low-priced issues and ignores the promising opportunities in this field.

Low Price Coupled with Speculative Capitalization: Speculatively capitalized enterprises, according to Graham's definition, are marked by a relatively large amount of senior securities and a comparatively small issue of common stock. Although the common share in most cases is sold at a low price, this is not always the case, as long as the market value of common stock comprises only a small part of the enterprise value.

Large Volume and High Production Cost Equivalent to Speculative Capital Structure: Showing three hypothetical copper companies, Graham shows how high production costs have the same effect as coupon payments for holders of senior securities. The simple effect is that the common stockholders have fewer earnings.

General Principle Derived. From the example, it can be derived that when the price of copper increases (which is good for all three copper-mining companies), there will be a higher profit increase percentage-wise for the high-cost producer than for the low-cost producer. This will be reflected in the share price. This is a very similar example to the purchaser of speculative capitalized common stock. If an investor anticipates that a company will pronounce improvement in sales or profit, the speculator can exploit the situation.

THE SOURCES OF INCOME

When we speak about a company's sources of income, we generally think in terms of the type of business. Different price-to-earnings multipliers have been used in different time periods but, because of the repeated variation, the security analyst must not use definitive rules in his valuations.

Of course, the better the track record and the more promising the prospects, the higher multiple a stock can be bought for. Still, the principle of price-earnings of 20 (introduced in Chapter 39) holds true in terms of it being classified in the investment price range, rather than that of speculation.

A Special Phase—Three Examples: Analysis must be conducted for the company based on the source of income from a specific asset, and not based on the general nature of the business.

1. *Northern Pipe Line Company:* Breaking down the sources of income for this company, it can be seen that a substantial part of the income comes from stable rental and interest earnings. This type of earnings must be evaluated based on the actual value of the asset-producing income. Income from bonds should also be valued on a higher basis, compared to the rather volatile pipeline business showing a negative trend.

2. *Lackawanna Security Company:* This company proved to be highly undervalued when its sources of income were examined more closely. As with Northern Pipe Line Company, a big part of the earnings was derived from bonds.

3. *Tobacco Products Corporation of Virginia:* This company was traded at a price-earnings of 10. All income came from a 99-year lease given to a high-quality company that could meet the obligation without question. This made the source of income from Tobacco Products Company of Virginia equivalent to a high-grade investment bond, and on this basis the company would be deemed undervalued.

Relative Importance of Situations: The above mentioned situations are relatively rare; however, they occur sufficiently to give this discussion practical value.

Two Lines of Conduct Suggested: The first point that can be derived from these examples is that the discussion gives an opportunity for the security analyst to detect undervaluation and profit from it. The second point is that, from the standpoint of the business owners, the whole arrangement might be wrong. For all three cases, there is the underlying problem that production and manufacturing companies have employed their capital in the ownership of high-grade bonds.

Illogical arrangements such as these should be recognized by the owners, who should insist that they be regulated—which, indeed, eventually happened for all of these companies. In the Northern Pipe Line Company example, capital not required for the pipeline business was realized and distributed back to the owners.

The situations we have just analyzed call for us to transfer our attention from the income statement to the balance sheet. This way we can analyze what the company does with the money they retain as earnings. This is next.

Part VI
Balance Sheet Analysis.
Implications of Asset Values

Chapter 42—Summary

Balance Sheet Analysis
Significance of Book Value

Graham starts this chapter by saying that Wall Street does not give enough attention to the balance sheet, listing five areas in which the balance sheet can provide guidance for the investor.

Book value of common stocks is defined and discussed, including the implication of preferred stocks. Graham also speaks about the practical use of book value. Although originally used to measure the value of a company, it is no longer as simple as that. As an example, he mentions that various accounting techniques can easily manipulate the book value; hence it would make no sense to make this equivalent to the value of the company. Graham presents some extraordinary cases with vast differences between book value and market price, and again concludes that the book value is not solely an indicator of value.

At the end of this chapter, Graham discusses whether he can make any recommendations about applying the book value of common stock. Graham believes that the only true recommendation is for the investor to know what he is doing when investing, and be secure in the knowledge that he/she is acting sensibly.

Chapter 42—Outline

Wall Street gives insufficient attention to the balance sheet. Graham believes that this is a mistake. What the balance sheet can provide is guidance for the investor, as follows:

1. It shows how much capital is invested in the business.
2. It reveals the ease or stringency of the company's financial condition; i.e., the working-capital position.
3. It contains the details of the capitalization structure.
4. It provides an important check of the validity of reported earnings.
5. It supplies the basis for analyzing the sources of income.

The book value of a stock is a somewhat simple measure, but it is often defined in different manners. It is customary to restrict the book value to the tangible assets, and not include intangible assets such as goodwill, trade names, patents, franchises, leaseholds. This is also why book value is often referred to as the "asset value," and sometimes as the "tangible asset value," to make it clear that intangibles are not included. In the case of common stocks and book value, it is also frequently termed as "equity."

- Note: In general, Graham does not place much value on intangibles, which is also why he wants these to be deducted from calculating the book value. Warren Buffett is of another opinion, and very often today you will see intangibles included. In this situation, the book value of a share is simply Equity / Number of shares outstanding. Here, equity is simple: All assets minus liabilities. As this book is based on Graham's work, his opinion will prevail.

Computation of Book Value: The book value per share of a common stock is found by adding up all the tangible assets, subtracting all liabilities and stock issues ahead, and dividing that by the number of shares.

Here, Graham provides a formula that can be used as a shortcut in many instances:

$$\frac{Common\, Stock + Surplus\, items - Intangibles}{Number\, of\, shares\, outstanding}$$

Surplus items would include retained earnings, premiums on stock issues, and various reserves.

Treatment of Preferred Stock When Calculating Book Value of Common Stock: In calculating the assets available for the common stock, the value of preferred stock must be subtracted. Ordinarily, this will be the par or stated value of the preferred stock as it appears in the balance sheet. In most cases, the result will be sufficiently accurate. That said, arbitrary values can also be found, and what Graham suggests is that we value preferred shares at par value plus back-end dividend payments and compare that to the market price. Whatever is highest (or most conservative) should be used.

Calculation of Book Value of Preferred Stocks: When calculating the book value of a preferred stock issue, it is treated as a common stock, as shown in the equation above, and junior issues are left out.

Current-Asset Value and Cash-Asset Value: In addition to the concept of book value, two similar concepts are also presented: current asset value and cash asset value.

The current asset value of a stock consists of the current assets alone, minus all liabilities and claims ahead of the issue. It excludes not only the intangible assets but also fixed and miscellaneous assets (various assets of value not related to the business, such as coin collections and artwork) as well. For a production company, it could look like this:

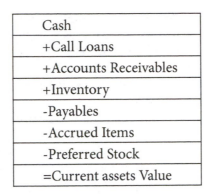

Cash
+Call Loans
+Accounts Receivables
+Inventory
-Payables
-Accrued Items
-Preferred Stock
=Current assets Value

- Note: The reason for this tedious calculation is that this is a prerequisite to fully understanding the concepts presented in the following chapter. Here, the current asset value is not properly defined.

The cash asset value of a stock consists of the cash assets alone, minus all liabilities and claims ahead of the issue. Cash assets, other than cash itself, are defined as those directly equivalent to and held in place of cash (such as certificates of deposit, marketable securities at market value).

Practical Significance of Book Value: The book value of a common stock was originally the most important element in a company's financial overview. The intention was to show the value of the business, but since it is far from reality, the carrying value (the number you can read from the balance sheet) has lost its significance. In most cases, the assets could not be sold at that value, and furthermore the figure is not justified by the earnings.

Also, the practice of writing up the book value of the fixed property, or cutting it down to nothing in order to avoid depreciation charges has made the book value have questionable application.

Graham lists four companies where there is a huge difference between the book value and the market price, and concludes that, be it in normal or extraordinary cases, the book value, at face-value, is not a business valuation measure.

Financial Reasoning vs. Business Reasoning: Graham argues that there is a vast difference between financial thought and ordinary business thought. If a businessman were offered 5% interest with a payout of $10,000, his first mental process would be to multiply the asked price by 20, and thus establish a proposed value of $200,000 for the entire undertaking. The rest of his calculation revolves around whether or not the business was a "good buy" at $200,000.

This elementary approach of understanding, *what the business is selling for,* is rarely predominant in the stock market. Of the thousands who "invested" in General Electric in 1929-1930 probably only an infinitesimal number had any idea that they were paying on the basis of about 2½ billion dollars for the company. Of this, over two billion represented a premium above the money actually invested in the business.

Recommendation: Even though Graham is very skeptical about using book value, he still believes that the book value deserves at least a fleeting glance before buying or selling shares. Before completely rejecting the use of book value, he argues that one needs to understand the idea behind it.

A stock buyer should know that the value of the stock is completely related to the business in question, and what he gets from his money will be in terms of tangible resources. A business that sells at a premium does so because it earns a large return compared to its capital. This large return attracts competition, and, generally speaking, it is not likely to continue indefinitely. Conversely, a business selling at a large discount because of abnormally low earnings should restore normal earnings for the opposite reasons. Although this might be a valid theory, Graham does not believe that it happens with enough certainty and speed for the book value to be a governing common stock selection.

Here, Graham also mentions that companies with high levels of intangibles might be less prone to competition, and that small companies in general are likely to show a more rapid rate of growth.

On the whole, he still finds no satisfactory rules about book value in relation to market price. The only strong recommendation is already made, and that is for the purchaser to know what he is doing on this score, and be satisfied in his own mind that he is acting sensibly.

Chapter 43—Summary

Significance of The Current Asset Value

This chapter continues to address the current asset value which was introduced in the previous chapter. Graham argues that this figure might be more important than the book value, and sets up three theses for this discussion.

While the liquidation value in theory can be calculated as assets minus liabilities, these numbers cannot be taken at face value. The rule is that all liabilities are real but the value of assets must be questioned. Here, some rules of thumb are provided for evaluating different categories of assets. Using White Motor Company as an example, Graham finds that the current asset value is a rough index of the liquidation value.

Graham investigates the second thesis by looking at stocks selling below the liquidation value. He does this to demonstrate the importance of the balance sheet. As there is no sound argument for why a company should be priced below the liquidation value, the management should either liquidate the company or investigate the disparity more closely, aiming to increase the market price.

Through his third thesis, Graham concludes that cheap stocks, with low current earnings and low price-to-current asset values, can be bought under the right circumstances where earnings can be expected to increase. Graham lists five scenarios. He also argues that the best time to go into these bargain investment stocks is when the stock market is not selling too high or too low.

Chapter 43—Outline

The current asset value of a common stock is more likely to be an important figure than the book value, which also includes the fixed assets.

In order to examine these, Graham establishes the following theses:

1. The current asset value is generally a rough index of the liquidating value.

2. A large number of common stocks sell for less than their current asset value and therefore sell below the amount realizable in liquidation.

3. The phenomenon of many stocks selling persistently below their liquidating value is fundamentally illogical. It means that a serious error is being committed, either: (a) in the judgment of the stock market, (b) in

the company's management policies, or (c) in the stockholders' attitude toward their property.

Liquidating Value: The liquidating value of an enterprise is the money the owners would receive, in theory, if they sold all assets and paid off all debt in the company. They might sell all or part of it to someone else, or they might turn the various kinds of assets into cash. Such liquidations are an everyday occurrence in the field of private business, but not for public companies.

Realizable Value of Assets Varies with Their Character: In reality, a company's balance sheet does not provide exact information about the liquidation value, but it does supply useful clues and hints. The first rule is that liabilities are real but the value of the assets must be questioned. This means that all true liabilities shown on the books must be deducted at their face amount. The value of the assets, however, must vary according to the character. Cash, for instance, is worth the carrying value, while inventory might only be worth 50-75% compared to the market price.

Object of this calculation: Applying a general rule of thumb for a real-life company, it can be seen that the stock was undervalued as it sold for less than the company's cash holding - even after deducting all liabilities. The aim of using current asset value as a liquidation measure is not to find the exact liquidation number, but to establish a rough estimate.

Note: Many modern readers believe these types of scenarios don't exist in the 21st century stock market, but that is a false claim. During the crash in 2008, numerous public companies sold on the exchange for less than their cash holdings.

Current Asset Value—a Rough Measure of Liquidation Value: Looking at a real-life company, one should consider the various types of asset that this specific company owns when calculating the liquidation value (inventory for canned goods can be valuated different than fresh fruit). For White Motor Company, Graham finds an estimated liquidation value of $31 per share, and correspondingly calculates the current asset value at $34. Based on this, Graham concludes that the first thesis mentioned at the beginning of the chapter holds true.

Prevalence of Stocks Selling below Liquidating Value: Some years, stocks sell at really low prices. At some time in 1932, over 40% of all the industrial companies listed on the New York Stock Exchange were quoted at less than their net current assets. Also at that time, a considerable number actually sold for less than their cash asset value. That actually means that the owner would profit more by shutting the company down than selling equity on a going concern basis.

One reason for the very low valuation is the high emphasis put on the income statement. A company with no current earnings will be considered highly negative by the stock market. The seller might not know he/she were disposing their interest in the company below liquidation value. This also explains the second thesis.

Logical Significance of this Phenomenon: The issue of the phenomenon just discussed may be summarized in the form of a basic principle: *When a common stock sells persistently below its liquidating value, then either the price is too low or the company should be liquidated.*

Two corollaries may be deduced from this principle:

Corollary I. Such a price should incite the stockholders to question whether it is in their interest to continue the business.

Corollary II. Such a price should incite the management to take all proper steps to correct the obvious disparity between market quotation and intrinsic value, including a reconsideration of its own policies and a frank justification to the stockholders of its decision to continue the business.

There can be no sound economic reason for a stock to continuously sell below the liquidation value.

Twofold Application of Foregoing Principle: The first application is that the low price offers an attractive opportunity to buy. The second is that the management should investigate mistaken policies going forward.

ATTRACTIVENESS OF SUCH ISSUES AS COMMITMENTS

Common stocks in this category almost always have an unsatisfactory trend of earnings. If the profits had been increasing steadily, the shares would obviously not sell at such low a price. There is a range of potential developments which may result in establishing a higher market price:

1. The creation of earning power that moves in lock-step with the company's assets (for instance from a general improvement in the industry or a change in the company's operating policies).

2. A sale or merger, because some other concern is able to utilize the resources to better advantage and hence can pay at least liquidating value for the assets.

3. Complete or partial liquidation.

Examples of the Effect of Favorable Developments on Such Issues:

General Improvement in the industry: When the textile business improved, the share of Pepperell increased more than eightfold in just two years.

Changes in Operating Policies: Examples of changes in operating policies for a

company could be new lines of products, new sales methods, and reorganizing phases of production.

Sale or Merger: White Motor Company was suffering heavy losses and was selling at a price lower than the liquidation value. The big cash holding was found interesting by an acquiring company, and the sales price was based on the current asset value.

Complete Liquidation: Investors of Mohawk Mining Company received 2½ times the cost of the shares when it was decided to completely liquidate the company. The liquidation value proved to be identical with the current asset value, and could be directly derived from the balance sheet.

Partial Liquidation: Sometimes an effective higher market value can be created by partially liquidating parts of the business and distributing that wealth out to the shareholders.

Discrimination Required in Selecting Such Issues: There is no doubt that stocks selling well below their liquidation value provides undervalued securities—and consequently profitable opportunities for purchase. Regardless, the securities analyst should exercise as much discrimination as possible when selecting between the prospects.

He can lean toward the five developments listed above if it is deemed that they may occur. Also, he can look at satisfactory current earnings and dividend, or a high average earning power in the past. The analyst will avoid companies that are losing current assets at a rapid rate and showing no sign of fixing the problem.

Examples: During the Depression, Hupp Motors lost 60% of current assets. The risk of losing the remaining current assets over market price is high. Manhattan Shirt, on the other hand, suffered a decline of just 10% in current assets during the difficult times, and had improved cash assets through liquidation of receivables and inventories. Clearly these two companies must be put in different categories in terms of investment options.

Bargains of This Type: Common stocks that (1) are selling below their liquid asset value, (2) are apparently in no danger of dissipating these assets, and (3) have formerly shown a large earning power on the market price, may be said to belong to a class of *investment bargains*. They are worth more than they are selling for, and there is a good chance that this will soon be reflected in the market price.

At their low price, these bargain stocks enjoy a high degree of safety, meaning a relatively small risk or loss of principal. It should be pointed out, however, that investors in such bargain issues should bear in mind the general market conditions at the time. The stock price in general should preferably be neither too high nor too low. If it is too high, the next drop will affect the bargain stock almost as severely as other stocks. If it is too low, the discount would allow for buying picks at very low prices.

A Common Stock Representing the Entire Business Cannot Be Less Safe than a Bond Having a Claim to Only a Part Thereof: This statement may sound abstract at first, as it has been common knowledge that bonds are safer than stocks. But a deeper understanding of the balance sheet for two different companies can explain the relationship.

Shawmut Association is capitalized only by stocks. Buying into the company at the current price level, the assets cover the share price 180% (you can think of this as a low price-book value of 100/180 = 0.55). In addition to this great protection, the stock also represents the entire ownership of the company's value.

Shawmut Bank Investment Trust is capitalized with both bonds and stocks. The bonds are protected only by 122% of their market price in assets. Furthermore, the bond holders' interest is limited to the principal amount of the bond.

To further explain the relationship about security in various capitalization formats, American Laundry Machine is introduced. This company traded very low compared to the earnings and equity in the company. Also, the earnings record was sound. According to Graham, Wall Street would gladly buy bonds issued from this company, but not stocks, due to safety issues. The argument was that the company would have to pay coupon payments to the bond holders, while the dividend payments were unsecure.

Here, Wall Street confuses the temporary consistency of income with the principle of safety. Dividends paid out to stockholders would not make the stock any safer. What is happening is that the stockholders turn over their own property. A rational stock owner would not surrender complete ownership for a limited claim and 5-6% returns on the investment.

Chapter 44—Summary

Implications of Liquidating Value Stockholder-Management Relationships

In this chapter, Graham examines the relationship between the stockholder and the management, focusing on situations where the market price is below the liquidation value. It might seem obvious that it would be profitable to buy into such a cheap venture, as the management could simply shut down the business and make a profit for the stockholder. While there is no reason in general to distrust the management, it must be understood that their interests may not be wholly consistent with those of the stockholder.

While directors have the controlling function of management, the investor must understand that they are also paid employees and often have strong ties to the chief executives. Independent of the directors, the investor must therefore always scrutinize areas where there might be conflict of interest. Salaries and bonuses are examples.

It is the stockholders' decision as to whether the business should continue—not the management's decision. In events where the liquidation value is higher than the stock price, this question logically arises, and the director must supply the argument as to why the company should potentially continue. Other remedies for maintaining the business and limiting the risk for investors include a dividend policy at least equivalent to the liquidation value; or returning all excess cash to the shareholders.

Using cash to conduct share buybacks can, in some situations, lead to financial distress and omission of dividends. When this happens, it can collapse the market price and becoming an unreasonable burden to the shareholders. This is especially true in the case of share buybacks being conducted to favor management and not stockholders.

Chapter 44—Outline

There are two logical reasons Wall Street would not buy into a stock selling below the liquidation value. The first is that the company cannot earn a satisfactory profit, and the second that it is not going to liquidate. We saw in the previous chapter that we could often reject the first statement, as there were several ways to make a reasonable return on capital in the future; however, some skepticism to the market price is justified.

Graham then raises the question about the second statement: "Why is it that, no matter how poor a corporation's prospects may seem, its owners permit it to remain in business until its resources are exhausted?" This is a discussion of the relationship between the value of securities, and the intelligence and alertness of those who own them

Typical Stockholder—Apathetic and Docile: It is a notorious fact that the typical American stockholder is not critical toward the board of directors. He rarely thinks of asserting his individual rights as an owner of the business and as an employer. The result is that the effective control of many, perhaps most, large American corporations is not governed by the stockholders, but by a small group - "the management." Quoting a book by Berle and Means, Graham finds that there is no guarantee that this group will work on behalf of the stockholders—perhaps quite the opposite in some cases.

Plausible but Partly Fallacious Assumptions by Stockholders: While the stockholder might not agree that he surrenders his right to having the company operated solely in his interest, Graham argues that the investor might base this on wrong assumptions. These wrong assumptions would include:

1. The management knows more about the business than the stockholders do, and therefore its judgment on all matters of policy is to be accepted.

2. The management has no interest in or responsibility for the prices at which the company's securities sell.

3. If a stockholder disapproves of any major policy of the management, his proper move is to sell his stock.

Assumed Wisdom and Efficiency of Management Not Always Justified: These statements are not completely wrong, and the half-truth makes them even more dangerous. While management typically knows its business very well, it is not true that it will always recognize and adopt the policies most beneficial to the shareholder.

Interests of Stockholders and Officers Conflict at Certain Points: In some situations, the management may explicitly have interests in conflict with those of the shareholders.

1. Compensation to officers—Salaries, bonuses, options to buy stock.

2. Expansion of the business—Involving the right to larger salaries and the acquisition of more power and prestige by the officers.

3. Payment of dividends—Should the money earned remain under the control of the management or pass into the hands of the stockholders?

4. Continuance of the stockholders' investment in the company—
   Should the business continue as before, although unprofitable,
   or should part of the capital be withdrawn, or should the
   business be wound up completely?

5. Information to stockholders—Should those in control be able
   to benefit through having information not generally given to
   stockholders?

For all of these questions, the decisions must be scrutinized by the investor
when examining the company. This is not the same as suggesting that
management is not trustworthy; it simply means that they should not be given
free rein. Likewise, a private employer hires people he can trust, but does not
let them determine their own pay.

**Directors Are Not Always Free from Self-interest in Connection with These
Matters:** In publicly owned corporations, it is the board of directors' job to
protect the interests of the stockholders. As directors are often paid officials,
and perhaps even have close ties to the chief executives, the stockholder
should remain critical and make an independent judgment.

Abuse of Managerial Compensation: Numerous cases have been seen where
management privileges have been abused. One severe example was the
management permitting themselves to buy the company's stock at lower
prices than the current market price. As it happened, the stock price dropped,
which caused the management to cancel the deal, and the money that the
management paid for the shares was returned.

Wisdom of Continuing the Business Should Be Considered: Management,
by definition, is reluctant to return capital to investors, even though the capital
might be more useful there. The reason is resource scarcity. For example if
the company has financial problems later, management might not have the
organic resource to pay the bills. Complete liquidation means the loss of the
job itself.

Whether or not the business should continue is a decision for stockholders,
not management. A logical reason to consider this is when the market price is
below the liquidation level. After all, that means that the market is wrong, or
that the management is wrong in keeping the enterprise alive.

Employees must also be heard, as it would be heartless to discuss a liquidation
solely based on the stockholders' pockets. If the reason for continuing the
business is to secure employment, employees should be made aware of this.
Whether or not a sacrifice of capital is reasonable in situations like this is
beyond the scope of this discussion.

Management May Properly Take Some Interest in Market Price for Shares: Management often avoids questions about the market price of their company's shares. While it is true that market fluctuation is not their responsibility, it is their job to establish a price that is not unduly high or low.

Various Possible Moves for Correcting Market Prices for Shares: If directors are convinced that continuation is preferable to liquidation, the reasons leading to this conclusion should be supplied. One solution to maintain the business and limit the risk for investors is a new dividend policy. The rate should be at least equivalent to the liquidation value, to ensure that stockholders do not to suffer as a result of this decision to keep the business alive. A third option could be to distribute excess cash back to stockholders. Graham provides examples of these options in practice.

Other Examples of Voluntary Liquidation: Liquidation of an unprofitable business with substantial assets is almost certain to realize more than the existing market price. The reason is that market prices are governed by earnings; the liquidation process is based on assets.

Repurchase of Share Pro Rata from Shareholders: If capital is no longer required, it can be advantageous to distribute it back though share buyback.

Abuse of Shareholders through Open-market Purchase of Shares: During the 1930–1933 Depression, repurchases of companies' shares were made with excess cash and without notice to the shareholder. It was deemed "in the interest of the corporation" to acquire the stock at the lowest possible price. Although in normal business it makes sense to buy assets as cheap as possible, the sellers of the stocks would suffer on behalf of those who hold on.

The company is obliged to act fairly towards the selling side. The desire to buy back shares might lead to the determination of or a reduction in dividend. This is a process hurtful to nearly all shareholders, and is only to the advantage of those who have retained their interest.

White Motor Company: When the company omitted dividends, the stock price almost collapsed. One reason they had to omit the dividend was due to the excessive share buy-backs the company had been conducting – which depleted their cash on-hand. An extraordinary amount of shares were bought back for the benefit of the employees, while the shareholders were left paying the price.

Westmore Coal Company: This company bought back its own shares when it sold at a price less than the cash asset alone. This low market price occurred because of the absence of earnings and irregular dividends. Graham believes that the excessive cash in the company (and there must have been excessive cash since the management were able to use it for share buyback) should have been distributed back to the stockholders as cash in the first place.

Summary and Conclusion: It is the stockholders who own the company; the officers are only paid employees. The directors are elected and virtually trustees, whose legal duty is to act solely on behalf of the business owners.

To make these general truths more effective in practice, the stock-owning public needs to be educated, to gain a clearer idea of the true interests of the stockholders.

Chapter 45—Summary

Balance Sheet Analysis (Concluded)

Graham starts this chapter by saying that the common purpose of balance sheet analysis is not to find bargain investments, but to detect financial weaknesses. It is a discipline that investors must practice before buying into new companies. Two basic rules are introduced. The first is that working capital ratio should be at least 2. The second is that the acid test ratio should be at least 1.

Next, various types of debt are discussed. It is found that a large banking debt is frequently a sign of financial weakness. If the security analyst finds debt that is soon to be repaid, either to the bank and/or to the bond holders, he must be careful. Graham points out that the speculative public does not always realize this, and can trade up the stock. The investor should therefore not trust the direction of the market price when assessing whether risk has increased or declined for such a company.

In this chapter, Graham finds three aspects that may be considered when comparing balance sheets over time. (1) The balance sheet can be used to check-up on earnings over time. He believes that, during a company analysis, the balance sheet tells a truer story than the reported earnings. (2) To determine the effect of losses (or profits) on the financial position of the company. Here, he finds that under certain conditions, a reported earnings loss can actually strengthen the company, and vice versa: an increase in reported earnings does not necessarily strengthen the financial position. (3) To trace the relationship between the company's resources and its earning power over a long period. This can only be achieved by conducting an exhaustive study. Graham does so for two companies, and the longer analysis period allows him to raise questions. The strength of this type of analysis is that it examines not only an individual company, but the profitability of the whole sector.

Chapter 45—Outline

So far, we have been looking at situations where the balance sheet exhibits a justified price other than the market price. The more common use of the balance sheet analysis is to detect the presence of financial weakness.

Careful buyers of securities need to scrutinize the balance sheet to check that cash is adequate, that current assets bear a suitable ratio to current liabilities, and whether there is any indication of refinancing problems.

WORKING-CAPITAL POSITION AND DEBT MATURITIES

Basic Rules Concerning Working Capital: for the working-capital ratio, a minimum of $2 of current assets for $1 of current liabilities was formerly regarded as a standard for industrial companies. A ratio below 2-to-1 or below the average in a group can lead to suspicion. While investors naturally favor a ratio in excess of this, it is hard to make an exact new rule, or to reject companies with a 2-to-1 ratio.

A second measure of financial strength is the "acid test," which requires that current assets - exclusive of inventories - should be at least equal to current liabilities. Failing these tests would make the security speculative and higher risk.

Exceptions and Examples: Archer-Daniels-Midland Company is an exception to the rule. Even though it failed the acid test, this was not a call for concern. While payables increased (lowering both the working-capital ratio and the acid ratio, as inventory increased), it represented normal seasoned practice in the industry.

Large Bank Debt Frequently a Sign of Weakness: It is rare that weak financial positions are created only by accounts payable. Weak financial positions are almost always characterized by the presence of bank loans or other debts due within a short timeframe.

Examples: It is hard to define how an investor or speculator should have looked at the balance sheet of New York Central. The substantial bank loans and bills payable were certainly not to be ignored. A more conservative investor would not have bought the stock, but at a very low price it may have constituted an attractive risk for the speculator.

Intercorporate Indebtedness: Current debt to a parent or affiliated company is theoretically as serious as any other short-term liability, but in practice the parent rarely makes the claim for payment.

Examples: Graham gives the example of a subsidiary with high current liabilities to its parent. Clearly that would look bad in terms of the working capital ratio; however, it did not prevent the company from paying out a preferred dividend.

The Danger of Early Maturing Funded Debt: When a large bond issue is due in the near future, it can create serious financial problems, especially when operating results are unfavorable. Maturing funded debt is a frequent cause of insolvency, and can be identified from the balance sheet.

Examples: Graham lists numerous examples of companies heading for financial distress due to early maturing funded debt, and notes how illogically the speculators behave in this situation. Despite being aware that the company needs costly refinancing or may even end up in receivership, speculators still buy into the stock.

Bank Loans of Intermediate Maturity: Very low interest rates have been used as a favorable condition to retire bond issues by taking loans repayable over a period of several years.

From the standpoint of security analysis, this bank credit resembles the short-term notes that were sold to the public as a familiar part of corporate financing. It is not a problem if the current assets are positioned strongly enough that loans can be paid off, or the earnings power is so large and dependable that it can refinance. However, if this is not the case, the security analyst must look at this as a potential threat to dividends or even solvency.

COMPARISON OF BALANCE SHEETS OVER A PERIOD OF TIME

This important part of security analysis acts in three ways:

1. As a check-up on the reported earnings per share.
2. To determine the effect of losses (or profits) on the company's financial position.
3. To trace the relationship between the company's resources and its earning power over a long period.

Check-up on Reported Earnings per Share, Via the Balance Sheet: Graham gives the example of U.S. Industrial Alcohol Company, over a 10-year period, to examine whether the reported earnings are indeed reflected in the balance sheet. It turns out that there is a big discrepancy, and that the earnings are not fully indicated on the balance sheet. The reason is that a variety of changes, such as mark-downs and write-offs, were made to surplus and not to the income statement.

- Note: this practice is no longer possible today.

Checking the Effect of Losses or Profit on the Company's Financial Position: Manhattan Shirt Company and Hupp Motors where already presented in Chapter 43. Comparing the balance sheet development between the two companies is an example of the second point mentioned above.

Taking Losses on Inventories May Strengthen Financial Position: Some losses are represented solely by a decline in the inventory account (which might only be worth 50-75% of the carrying value).

In fact, if the shrinkage in the inventory exceeds the losses, leading to an actual increase in cash or reduction in payables, it may then be proper to say that the company's financial position has been strengthened, even though it has been suffering losses.

On the basis of liquidation value, the investor in Manhattan Shirt Company would actually have *increased* the value during the depression as a result of the company turning assets into cash. Here we have the contrast between the indicators of the income statement showing losses, and the truer story told by the balance sheet.

Is Shrinkage in Value of Normal Inventory an Operating Loss? Graham does not directly answer his own question, but discusses the theoretical implication. While the inventory should be written down—for instance, due to a lower sales price—one might argue that the fixed assets should suffer a similar loss. The analyst should in theory be able to calculate earning power and make a "normal stock" basis for his analysis.

In reality, he does not have that sort of data, and therefore must use general and not exact allowances for the distortion effect of inventory price change.

Profits from Inventory Inflation: In the event of high inflation, in terms of accounting, the inventory will increase in value. For industrial companies, this could occur from speculative advances in commodity prices.

Examples: U.S. Rubber is an example of an increase in earnings, partly made from heavy expenditures on a plant and a dangerous expansion in inventory from 1919-1920, with high inflation. The investor, only looking at the increased reported earnings, would not have found this.

Long-Range Study of Earning Power and Resources

The third aspect is of restricted interest, since only an exhaustive study of a company's record and balance sheet analysis would justify the analysis.

I. UNITED STATES STEEL CORPORATION: ANALYSIS OF OPERATING RESULTS AND FINANCIAL CHANGES BY DECADE, 1903-1932

Balance sheet and income statement indicate dividend per decade.

The significance of Foregoing Figures: Having data divided into decades reveals something different than what we would see from a year-to-year review. For this company, the effect of World War I is very clear, and has added a big sum to the earnings. The rate of earnings of the investing capital has, however, declined in the last decade.

This raises the question of whether the end of the war turned the industry into a relatively unprofitable business, from a previously relatively prosperous one. It also raises the question of whether it was due to the high reinvestment, which led to overcapacity and consequently lower return.

Postscript: Looking back at the first question, the answer seems to be *yes*. Earnings were lacking for the whole industry.

II. SIMILAR ANALYSIS OF CORN PRODUCTS REFINING COMPANY, FEBRUARY 28, 1906 TO DECEMBER 31, 1935

Comment on the Corn Products Refining Company Exhibits: For this company, Graham again goes through the financial statements in a rather descriptive manner. It can also be seen that the war has contributed substantially to its earnings. The rate of return on invested capital, however, did not seem to be affected during the Depression years.

This conclusion was neither distorted by the deductions, write-downs, or depreciation charges. Based on his analysis of the financial statement, Graham does not suggest raising the same concern for the U.S. Steel Company.

Part VII
Additional Aspects of Security Analysis. Discrepancies Between Price and Value

Chapter 46—Summary

Stock-Option Warrants

In this chapter, Graham outlines three areas of warrants that he wants to examine. The first (1) is a description of warrants. Here, we learn that a warrant is a privilege to buy a common stock. We also learn that the stock purchase price is typically set higher than the current market price, and the duration of time often exceeds a year.

The second aspect examined is speculation for warrants (2), and Graham argues that it is the qualitative element that makes up the speculation. The value of quantitative elements can be measured much more easily, but it is the future earnings increase that can ultimately make the value tangible for the warrant holder.

Warrants can have a significant impact on the financial structure (3). In general, Graham does not like the idea of using warrants as a source of funding. It adds nothing that the issue of common stock couldn't do, and it dilutes the common stock value. Further, the indifferent public tends to disregard the issue of these warrants, which leads to artificially high market valuation.

Chapter 46—Outline

Previously, a stock-option warrant was something that was attached to a bond or a preferred stock, and carried privileges. It was not seen as an independent instrument and as an important part of the capitalization. Today, opinions are reversed, and it has even turned into a popular medium for speculators. This chapter will look at the stock-option warrant as a separate financial instrument, and can be divided into three categories:

1) Description
2) Technical characteristics of warrants as vehicles of speculation
3) Their significance as a part of the financial structure

DESCRIPTIVE SUMMARY

A (detachable) option warrant is a transferable right to buy stock. The right can be described in detail by the following information:

(1) the kind of stock, (2) the amount, (3) the price, (4) the method of payment, (5) the duration of the privilege, and (6) anti-dilution provisions.

Type of Stock Covered by the Privilege. Nearly all option warrants can be converted to common stock for the issuing company. Very few have rights that apply to preferred shares. Warrants have no right to receive interest, dividends or payments on account of principal, nor do they have the right to cast any vote.

Resemblance to Subscription "Right": Warrants are in many ways similar to the subscription rights issued by the corporation to stockholders in connection with the sale of additional stock. Differences occur, however, in terms of the exercised price and the time period. Subscription rights will typically always be exercised unless the stock price drops substantially, and it will generally happen within the 60 days that the rights typically run. Warrants, on the other hand, are seldom exercised in such a short period of time, as the stock purchase price is typically set higher than the current stock price at the time of issue. The duration is most often longer than a year.

Method of Payment. Most option warrants require payment of the subscription price in cash.

Basis of Trading in Warrants. Option warrants are bought and sold in the market in the same way as common stocks. The standard rule of a warrant is the right to buy one share of the stock.

Examples of Warrants Issued for Various Purposes:
- A. Attached to senior securities.
- B. As compensation to underwriters.
- C. As compensation to promoters and management.
- D. Issued in a merger or reorganization plan, in exchange for other securities.
- E. Attached to an original issue of common stock.
- F. Sold separately for cash.

WARRANTS AS A VEHICLE OF SPECULATION

Option warrants possess the same general characteristics as low-priced common stocks, and are in essence a long-term call upon the business. You can compare the relationship between a warrant and a common stock to the relationship between a common stock and a speculative senior security.

The Qualitative Element: The attractiveness of a warrant is to a degree determined by a speculative qualitative part, which is the nature of the businesses. While a lot can be said about the quantitative element, such as a warrant duration and price, the analyst cannot be expected to predict how companies will perform in the future. This leads to a speculative element. Since the value of a warrant will only materialize from an increase in earnings, the prospects of increased earnings would make the warrant more attractive than its stability.

Quantitative Considerations: Importance of Low Price. It is easier to look at the attractiveness of warrants from a quantitative standpoint. The desirable qualities are: low price, long duration, and option price close to the market. The most important quality is that of its low price. Still, Graham feels that an option warrant has speculative attractiveness only if it possesses all three desirable qualities.

Low Relative Price Importance: The price of the warrant should not only be low; it should also be relative to the price of the common stock.

Examples: To demonstrate this point on low relative price importance, Graham looks at a company with a call of stock at $25; the stock price was $31 and the price of the warrant was $6. In other words, the warrant was selling at parity. Any rise in the price of the stock would lead to a proportional higher increase in price for the warrant.

Technical Advantages Often Absent. When stock prices are high, warrants generally follow suit, both in absolute and relative terms. The same can be said when stock trades at a low level. The implication is that the technical advantage mentioned above is often absent.

WARRANTS AS PART OF THE CAPITALIZATION STRUCTURE

The basic fact about an option warrant is that it represents something that has been taken away from the common stock. This is because benefitting from a warrant is much more restricted than a common stock. The equation for this is:

Cost of Common Stock + Cost to own Warrant = Value of the Common Stock alone (since there are no warrants)

Warrants Represent a Subtraction from the Related Stock. As warrants give rights to buy stock at a given price level, when that price level is reached, earnings will be diluted for the common stockholder because they still must account for the cost to acquire the warrant.

Note: In this section, Graham is referring to the dilution of the overall equity in the business. From an individual investor's stand-point, owning a warrant can absolutely add value when held and sold above it's parity value with the common stock.

A Dangerous Device for Diluting Stock Values. The option warrant is a dangerous device because it dilutes common-stock values. Graham argues that stockholders view the issuance of warrants with indifference, failing to realize that part of their future equity is being taken from them. In this case, the common shareholders value stocks similarly whether warrants are outstanding or not.

A *Reductio ad Absurdum*. The original issue of common stock carrying warrants to buy additional stock does not give stockholders anything more than they would have without the warrant. Further, it violates an obvious rule of sound corporate financing. A properly managed business sells additional stock only when new capital is needed.

Chapter 47—Summary

Cost of Financing and Management

When an investment bank issues securities for a company, it is both a complex and costly process. In this chapter, Graham goes into detail discussing what the investor is actually paying for when buying common stock at a premium. He illustrates this with an example in which the public is paying 25-30% for underwriting, warrant issues, and salaries to management. While not giving any direct number for an appropriate premium, it is clear that he thinks that many investment bankers are paid too much.

Graham advocates much stricter regulation to protect the public, as even full disclosure would only help the most experienced of analysts. What can be observed is that management compensation has not been fully disclosed, and stock option warrants have been an unfortunate instrument to dilute earnings for the company on behalf of the operating management.

Chapter 47—Outline

To show the details of the financing involved in the issue of shares, Graham presents a real-life company. The company's stock was sold at $34 a share but the money it received for the sale was $31. Also, half of the share issued was issued to unnamed recipients. These were presumably promoters, investment managers, and the management.

Cost of Management: Three Items. Buyers of the stock at $34 per share were asked to pay for the management in three ways:

1. The $3 difference between the price the investor paid and the price the company paid. While this money would go to the investment banker as an underwriter's fee, in reality that premium is paid in the belief that the management was worth the difference.

2. The issue of the warrants had in effect taken value away from the common stockholder, of one-third of the appreciation.

3. The salaries the officers were to receive plus additional taxes.

The three items together may be said to absorb between 25 and 30% of the amount contributed by the public.

What was received for the price paid? Graham discusses what the stockholders got in return for the premium they paid. The board of directors had specific knowledge that was considered worth having; however, there were two limitations to this. The first was that they were not obliged to devote themselves solely to the company. The second limitation came from the projected activities. As the company operated only in the petroleum field, there was less need for managerial skills, once funds were allocated to the initial acquisitions.

Position of Investment Banking Firms in This Connection: Prior to the 1920's, the sale of stock to the public by reputable houses of issue was governed by three important principles:

1. The enterprise must be well established and possess satisfactory records and financial exhibits to justify the purchase of the shares at the issue price.

2. The investment banker must act primarily as the representative of the buyers of the stock, and he must deal at arm's length with the company's management.

3. The compensation taken by the investment banker must be reasonable. It represents a fee paid by the corporation for the service of raising capital.

These rules of conduct were established to ensure responsible and fair stock financing.

Developments since 1929: A few years after the Depression, some stock financing operations were less ethical (similar to the example at the beginning of the chapter), but recently this has improved, and most are conducted in accordance with the rules outlined above.

New Role of Such Investment Bankers: The investment banker has two tasks that might conflict. He makes a deal with the originator of the enterprise, and then he makes a separate deal with the public, to raise the funds he has promised the business.

While he is entitled to be rewarded for his efforts, the extent of his compensation may induce a change in the relationship to the public. Is he their agent or is he serving as a promoter? If the latter is the case, the public is certain to suffer. That said, full disclosure of the deal might only benefit the most skilled of investors anyway, and not the public, who do not possess the necessary skills to understand the information.

Examples: To prove his point, Graham introduces two companies that were financed in 1936 and 1939, for which the public paid a high premium to the investment bankers and the management. He also shows that it requires working through a very detailed and tedious procedure in order to understand exactly how much they paid, and what they paid for.

Should the Public Finance New Ventures? It might be reasonable to ask whether the cost involved for the public for financing new ventures makes it worthwhile for them. Graham thinks that this is essential to American progress; however, he advocates more drastic legislation.

Blue-Sky Promotions: In the "Good ol' days," stock promoters would try to sell anything. Potential clients were essentially buying a "blue sky." Due to tight regulation, this is no longer possible. Instead, the promoter selects a real enterprise—one he can sell at much more than its fair value. If all of the desired elements are present, and he can sell an asset worth $1 for $5, the law can be respected and the public exploited. These promotions are especially fitting for any new industry that catches the public's eye.

Repercussions of Unsound Investment Banking. The investment bankers' process of issuing stocks and other securities has had repercussions in the field of corporate management. Whether inflated management salaries are justified remains open for debate, and the answer depends on the unique capabilities that management contributes towards the success of the company. But it is a fact that a substantial part of an enterprise's profits are distributed to operating managers, and that this is done without full disclosure. Stock option warrants have proven to be an excellent instrument for that purpose.

Chapter 48—Summary

Some Aspects of Corporate Pyramiding

In this chapter, Graham explains how a holding company can be used for pyramiding. The intention is to generate high profits by controlling a variety of companies, but at the same time pay little or essentially no capital to do so. The key is to use a very high degree of leverage.

Graham lists four reasons why pyramiding is harmful for the security-buying public. One main concern is that the capital structure leads to speculation. Another concern is that it is very hard to study the financial reports; pyramiding allows for various accounting techniques that can distort earnings, book value, and dividend returns. This will in turn artificially increase the price of the holding company, so that new issues can also be quoted at inflated prices.

Chapter 48—Outline

Pyramiding in corporate finance is the creation of a speculative capital structure by means of a holding company or a series of holding companies. By such a construction, the organizers can control a large business with only little or no capital. Often the intention is to "cash in" speculative profits, and at the same time retain control.

Examples: Graham provides a real-life example of a company that was bought for $8,500,000 and financed by a note to seller for $6,500,000 with the remaining $2,000,000 paid in cash. The cash payment was bought from a bank, essentially meaning that almost no capital was needed.

Evils of Corporate Pyramiding. The pyramiding structure is harmful to the security-buying public from several standpoints.

1) It results in the creation and sale to investors of large amounts of unsound senior securities

2) The common stock of the governing holding companies is subject to deceptively rapid increases in earning power during favorable years, which can lead to disastrous public speculation

3) The position of control of someone who owns only little or no capital is bound to lead to irresponsible and unsound management

4) It allows for deceiving accounting techniques in terms of indicated earnings, dividend return, and book value. This will again lead to speculation

The last point will be looked at further.

Overstatement of Earnings. Holding companies can overstate their earnings power by valuing, at an artificially high prices, the stock dividends they receive from subsidiaries. Earning power can also be overstated using profits made from the sale of stock of subsidiary companies.

Distortion of Dividend Return. Stock dividends can be paid out with a market value exceeding current earnings. Graham notes that people regard the value of subscription rights (the right for existing shareholders to maintain their ownership by subscribing to new stock issues) equivalent to an income return on the common stock. This subscription can often be used, since the business model of these holding companies is to use their predominant position to expand. For the analyst, these rights are typically proven delusional.

Exaggeration of Book Value. The exaggeration of book value may occur in cases where a holding company owns most of the shares of a subsidiary, consequently making it possible to manipulate the small amount of stock remaining in the market. New issue of shares on the subsidiary can then be sold at the higher quotation, which is based on the book value of the holding company (sometimes called break-up value).

Exploitation of the Stock-Purchase-Warrant Device. The result of this process for American and Foreign Power Common, at its farthest point, in 1929, was absurd. A company with earnings of just $6,510,000 translated into a staggering market value of $1,560,000,000. One reason was that utility companies at the time were traded at 50 times earnings, but the common stock value only constituted about one-fifth of the market value. The remaining came from warrants. The high value was exploited to justify a high quotation on later issues.

Some Holding Companies Not Guilty of Excessive Pyramiding: Although pyramiding is usually effected by means of holding companies, not all holding companies are created for that purpose.

Legitimate reasons for their creation include: to permit unified and economical operations of separate units, to diversify investment and risk, and to gain certain technical advantages of flexibility and convenience. Any holding company should always be considered on its merits.

Speculative Capital Structure May be Created in Other Ways: Speculative capital structure does not only exist in the form of holding companies. Graham lists one example of a company that had a very speculative capital structure resulting from a substantial issue of preferred stocks.

Legislative Restraints on Pyramiding. The disastrous effects of the public utility pyramiding of the 1920s had made Congress take drastic actions. The

Public Utility Holding Company Act of 1935 required them ultimately to simplify their capital structures and to dispose of subsidiaries operating in non-contiguous territory.

Chapter 49—Summary

Comparative Analysis of Companies in The Same Field

In this chapter, Graham provides an outline of how an analyst can make an industry comparison. Studying a comparative analysis can give indications of whether one stock should be replaced by another in the same field. The reason can be either the performance or the price level.

Graham studies railroads, public utility and industrial companies in very general terms. For each category of businesses, a series of quantitative data can be derived, typically from the financial statements. While Graham both encourages and acknowledges this approach, a qualitative study may provide adequate reasons for differences that the statistics do not disclose. Among many reasons may be a poorer outlook or questionable management.

One fact that the analyst should be aware of when conducting his analysis is whether or not he is looking at a homogenous industry. Homogenous companies respond similarly to a change in business conditions. In this case, an industry comparison is considered more dependable.

Chapter 49—Outline

Statistical comparisons of companies in a given industry are more or less routine and part of the analyst's work. This process permits each company's records to be studied against a background of the industry as a whole. It shows if the security is under- or overvalued, or leads to the conclusion that, in a given field, one stock should be exchanged with another in the portfolio.

Next, Graham goes on to list as many as 32 numbers that the analyst can either find or calculate in the financial statements. They include everything from market capitalization, dividend rate, and seven-year average earnings.

FORM I. RAILROAD COMPARISON

Observations on the Railroad Comparison

Whether the average period should be seven years, shorter, or longer is an individual choice. In theory, it should be long enough to cover all cyclical fluctuations, but not so long that it includes data that are totally out of date.

Figures related to preferred stocks fall into two different classes, dependent on whether it involves a fixed-value investment or a speculative commitment.

The market price should be able to tell you which category it belongs to.

Speculative preferred shares should generally be analyzed similarly to common stock. It should be remembered, however, that a preferred stock is always less attractive showing the same earnings.

Limitation upon Comparison of Speculatively and Conservatively Capitalized Companies in the Same Field: The analyst must be aware of trying to draw conclusions to the relative attractiveness of two railroad common stocks when one is speculatively and the other is conservatively capitalized. They react differently to changes, and the advantage that one company may possess could be lost if conditions change.

Other Illustrations in Appendix: Graham finds that the practical approach of a comparative analysis of bonds and stock in the railroad industry can best be illustrated by an analysis he did himself, and should not be elaborated on any further.

Note: This very exhaustive analysis can be found in the appendix of the 1940 Edition.

FORM II. PUBLIC UTILITY COMPARISON

The public utility industry is practically the same as that for railroads; only a few numbers need to be changed. Variations in depreciation rates are equally as important as variations in the railroad study. When a wide difference is observed in the comparison, it should not be assumed that one company is conservative and another is not. This also means that if one public utility company looks more statistically appealing than another, studies must be conducted to assess its situation and how it might develop in favorable and unfavorable conditions.

FORM III. INDUSTRIAL COMPARISON (FOR COMPANIES IN THE SAME FIELD)

In the case of industrial comparison, a variety of aspects are different, and Graham lists as many as 38 numbers, which he divides into 7 different categories. The common denominator is that not only the income statement and balance sheet are of interest, but market capitalization, dividends, and earnings trends must be examined closely too.

Observations on the Industrial Comparison: To carry out a proper industry comparison, net earnings must be corrected for any known distortion or omission. This includes undistributed earnings and losses of subsidiaries. Depreciation rates should only serve to locate vast discrepancies, and not be used for exact comparisons.

It is not safe to rely on higher-than-average return on equity figures when compared to the industry, unless the same can be said about return on investment. If a company with poorer earnings shows a high sale compared to equity, it may allow for good speculative possibilities in the event of general business improvement.

While key ratios should also be calculated for the balance sheet, they are of limited interest unless they indicate either financial weaknesses, or the net current asset value is very high compared to the market price.

Example of the Use of Standard Forms: Graham shows the practicality of the industrial comparison procedure, analyzing two companies in the steel industry. A quantitative comparison easily shows the difference between companies, but Graham makes two general comments: first, the most recent numbers would require the most attention; and secondly, the analyst should aim to learn as much as possible about the underlying reasons for the difference in performance.

Study of Qualitative Factors Also Necessary. Graham continues his caution about solely trusting numbers. For instance, when one issue seems to be selling much too low in relation to another in the same field, there may be adequate reasons for this disparity that the statistics do not disclose. Among such valid reasons may be a definitely poorer outlook or questionable management.

While not entirely a qualitative factor, Graham goes on to discuss dividend return. He believes that a lower dividend return for a common stock should not ordinarily be considered as a strong offsetting factor, since the dividend is usually adjusted to the earning power within a reasonable period of time.

Although over-conservative dividend policies are sometimes followed for a considerable period, there is a well-defined tendency even in these cases for the market price to reflect the earnings power sooner or later.

Variations in Homogeneity Affect the Values of Comparative Analysis: The use of a comparison varies depending on the industry. If a group of companies are reacting similarly to a change in business conditions, they can be said to be "homogenous." One way to locate this is to look at past financial results and let these serve as an indicator of how the industry will react in the future.

Homogenous groups would include those in railroad, utilities, and larger oil companies. Makers of manufactured goods sold under advertised trademarks must generally be regarded as belonging to heterogeneous groups. Here, one company frequently prospers at the expense of its competitors.

As a general rule, the less homogeneous the industry, the more attention needs to be paid to the qualitative factors when making comparisons.

More General Limitations on the Value of Comparative Analysis: Graham again cautions the analyst not to look for an exact mathematical solution. The analyst must consider qualitative factors and perhaps also allow for the lack of homogeneity. The technique of comparative analysis may facilitate his task, but he must still expect to be wrong from time to time. Still, with intelligence and prudence, he should yield better results than the guesses of the typical stock buyer.

Chapter 50—Summary

Discrepancies Between Price and Value

In this chapter, Graham revisits many of the conclusions expressed previously in the book, this time with a more practical approach for the analyst. He starts out by suggesting two different methods for finding good investments. One is to make an industry comparison and closely investigate the best performers; another is to quickly glance over multiple corporate reports and scrutinize the most interesting.

Graham then looks at whether one can exploit the fact that bull markets sell too high and bear markets sell too low. He establishes objective criteria to determine the market, but finds that, even in hindsight, the practical implication of such a strategy has little practical use. The same can be said for bonds.

Graham argues that the analyst can always find interesting investment objects simply based on quantitative data. What is more difficult is the task of determining whether the qualitative factors justify the quantitative indications. The analyst should view the qualitative aspects of the business as being where the real bargain is made.

The analyst can also benefit from understanding when the market is overreacting. This happens, for instance, when dividend payout changes, mergers and acquisitions occur, and litigation is being processed. Very often, there is no fundamental argument behind market fluctuations. In the event of receivership, Graham also observes that stocks are traded too high, and bonds gradually decline in price, typically to the lowest level, just before a reorganization plan is introduced.

Chapter 50—Outline

So far, this book has provided various techniques of security analysis to determine whether a security is over- or undervalued. In reality, the processes by which the securities market arrives at its appraisals are frequently illogical and erroneous. Most of them can be traced to one or more of these three basic causes: exaggeration, oversimplification, and neglect.

This chapter and the next will review the securities market from a more practical standpoint. The security-analysis limitations faced in earlier chapters will now be addressed again, this time with the additional knowledge gained from successive chapters.

General Procedure of the Analyst. The procedure by which the analyst finds good investments involves hard and systematic work. There are two broad methods.

The first is to conduct a series of comparative analyses of industrial groups along the lines described in the previous chapter. Such studies will give a fair idea of the standard or usual characteristics of that industry; for example, if the analyst discovers that one company makes twice the earnings in relative terms to the industry, he will have a clue to work on. The same type of methodical inquiry may be applied to the field of bonds and preferred stocks.

The second general method consists of scrutinizing corporate reports. A quick glance over hundreds of such reports may reveal between five and ten that look interesting enough from the earnings or current asset standpoint.

Can Cyclical Swings of Prices Be Exploited? A difference between price and value that is very easy to understand is that of the recurrent broad swings of the stock market through boom and depression. It is a known fact that stocks are sold too expensive in bull markets and sold too low in bear markets. It would seem reasonable to ponder whether these practices can be exploited, since they can be anticipated.

One can set-up criteria to give an objective opinion of the price level of the stock market, then trade accordingly. While Graham argues the practicality of such a procedure is low, and under the Great Depression would have made heavy demands upon human fortitude, he still finds the idea appealing. The reason is by looking into such a procedure, one is more likely to buy at attractive intrinsic value levels.

"Catching the Swings" on a Marginal Basis Impracticable: The investor can afford to buy too soon and to sell too soon. In fact, he must expect to do both, as the market is practically impossible to time.

But the marginal trader is concerned with immediate results. He rarely succeeds, so the typical experience is temporary success ending in complete disaster. He buys because he thinks that the stock price will increase in value, not because it is cheap.

Bond prices tend to swing through cycles in somewhat the same way as stocks. It is frequently suggested that bond investors follow the policy of selling their holdings near the top of these cycles and repurchasing them near the bottom. In reality, there are no well-defined criteria to measure when high-grade bonds are either priced low or high, and it is doubtful that such timing can be anticipated.

Opportunities in "Secondary" or Little-Known Issues. When the market leaders are cheap, some of the less prominent common stocks are likely to be a good deal cheaper.

The Impermanence of Leadership. The composition of the market leader group varies greatly from year to year, especially in view of the recent shift of attention from past performance to assumed prospects. As an example of this, Graham highlights Great Atlantic and Pacific Tea Company. In 1938, it was traded at less than its liquidation value though it was the largest retailer in the US and had shown continued positive earnings. The reasons were threefold: chain-store tax threat, recent decline in earnings, and general market depression.

The real nature of the stock market is not to evaluate businesses, but rather to express its likes and dislikes, its hopes and fears, in the form of daily changing quotations. When we are dealing with something as elusive and nonmathematical as the evaluation of future prospects, we are generally led to accept the market's verdict as being better than anything that the analyst can arrive at.

Opportunities in Normal Markets. During a period when the market in general shows no definite signs of being too low or too high, stocks can still be found cheap on a statistical basis. These stocks generally fall into two classes:

1. Those showing high current and average earnings in relation to market price
2. Those making a reasonably satisfactory exhibit of earnings and selling at a low price in relation to net-current asset value. These companies will most often not be large and well known

It is easy to find stocks that are interesting from a statistical point of view. The more difficult task is that of determining whether the qualitative factors justify following the quantitative indications. That is ultimately what should provide the investor with sufficient confidence in the company's future to consider its shares a real bargain.

There are reasons why investment trusts typically have not bought into these companies. Firstly, they cannot buy and sell in large quantities; and secondly, the conviction of the qualitative factors is different. The main drawback of a small company is its vulnerability for loss of earning power. Larger companies will be less prone to this. The counter argument is that successful smaller companies can multiply in size more impressively than those already of enormous size.

Market Behavior of Standard and Nonstandard Issues: A close study of the market action of common stocks suggests:

1. Standard or leading issues almost always respond rapidly to changes in their reported profits—they tend to exaggerate the significance of year-to-year fluctuations in earnings.

2. The action of the less familiar issues depends largely upon the attitude of the professional market operators towards them. If there is interest in the issue, legitimate as well as speculative, the price will respond in an extreme fashion.

Relationship of the Analyst to Such Situations. When the general market appears dangerously overvalued to the analyst, he must exercise caution when it comes to unfamiliar common stocks. The same applies when stocks appear to be bargains. A severe decline in the general market will affect all stock prices adversely, and the less familiar issues may prove especially vulnerable.

Market Exaggerations Due to Factors Other than Changes in Earnings: *Dividend Changes.* While there is no doubt that a dividend increase is a favorable development, a large increase in stock prices based solely on this is absurd.

Mergers and Segregations: Studies into whether mergers and acquisitions aid in increasing earning power have in general indicated that no such effect can be found. Instead, there is reason to believe that the personal element in corporate management often stands in the way of advantageous consolidations. In light of this fact, it is surprising that the stock market tends to react so positively to mergers and acquisitions in the short run.

Litigation: A lawsuit of any significance is highly disliked by the stock market, often to an extent that is out of proportion to the impact of the case in question. Developments of this kind may offer real opportunities to the analyst.

Undervalued Investment Issues: Undervalued bonds and preferred stocks of investment caliber may be discovered in any period by means of thorough research. In many cases, the low price of a bond or preferred stock is due to a poor market, which in turn results from the small size of the issue. But this very small size may make for greater inherent security, as there is relatively more common stock to a small senior issue. Still, the price can be under par.

Price-Value Discrepancies in Receivership: Earlier, it was argued that one should not buy into a stock if it was likely to fall into financial difficulties. Here, Graham argues that the analyst can invest in securities after such difficulties have arisen, because senior securities have been found to sell at too low prices. Cases of reorganization, and other situations where liquidation or sale to outside interest, ultimately results in a cash distributions that can produce attractive analytical opportunities.

Price Patterns Produced by Insolvency: Certain price patterns tend to occur, especially if the receivership tends to take a long time. First, there is a tendency for the stock issue to sell too high, not only toward the bond issue, but also to their estimated value. For bond issues, the price typically declines over time, reaching the lowest point just before a reorganization plan is ready to be announced.

Remaining in close touch with such situations and finding securities that are selling far below the intrinsic value should be profitable. As in all analytical situations, there is no need to spend too much time thinking about the timing of the purchase.

Opportunities in Railroad Trusteeships: In the years following 1932 and the following year, a large part of the country's railroad mileage fell into the hands of the trustee. This provided the shrewd investors with interesting opportunities as it put pressure on the price levels of the securities.

Chapter 51—Summary

Discrepancies Between Price and Value (Continued)

This chapter continues where Chapter 50 left off, but shifts the focus onto senior securities rather than common stocks. Graham divides the securities into two classes: seasoned, which are favored issues well known by the public, and unseasoned, which are the opposite. Unseasoned issues are generally more vulnerable to dissatisfactory development.

Securities can be evaluated by comparison, and it is often done this way, even when the aim is to find the discrepancy between price and value. Graham nevertheless recommends that the investor doesn't only purchase the best alternative. One recommendation is that the issue to be bought should be attractive in its own right.

Chapter 51—Outline

The practical distinction in the previous chapter about leading and secondary stock has its counterparts in the field of senior securities. A seasoned issue may be defined as an issue of a company that is long and favorably known to the investment public. Seasoned and unseasoned issues tend at times to follow different patterns on the market:

> 1. The price of seasoned issues is often maintained despite a considerable weakening of their investment position.

> 2. Unseasoned issues are very sensitive to adverse developments of any nature. Hence they often fall to prices far lower than seem to be warranted by their statistical exhibit.

Price Inertia of Seasoned Issues: The typical investor buys on reputation rather than by analysis and he holds on stubbornly to what he has bought. Even a small decline in price attracts buyers.

Vulnerability of Unseasoned Issues. Unseasoned issues are almost entirely in the industrial field. The prices follow the statistical characteristics fairly closely, without being influenced by their popularity. If the earnings power is maintained, the unseasoned issue would also maintain the price, but even slight dissatisfactory development will lead to severe price decline.

Because of price sensitivity to unfavorable development, it would seem that price could fall very low, and thereby create attractive opportunities for purchase. While this is true, one should also exercise caution, as the price decline does not solely originate from a lack of knowledge.

Unseasoned Industrial Issues Rarely Deserve an Investment Rating. Unseasoned industrial issues should only be bought on an admittedly speculative basis. This requires in turn that the market price be low enough to permit a substantial rise, typically below 70.

Discrepancies in Comparative Prices: It is easier to determine whether issue A is better than issue B, than to determine whether issue A in its own right is a good investment. Past interest coverage should be calculated and analyzed, but keeping in mind that the security is being bought for future performance.

Graham then gives two recommendations for selecting an issue to purchase. (1) The issue to be bought is attractive in its own right, or (2) there is a definite contractual relationship between the two issues in question.

For the first recommendation, a qualitative analysis must also be carried out, to evaluate the future earning power. The second is examined next.

Comparison of Definitely Related Issues. When the issues examined are definitely related, we have a different situation. An exchange can then be considered solely from the standpoint of the respective merits within the given situation. This means that the responsibility for entering into or remaining in the situation need not be assumed by the analyst.

Other and Less Certain Discrepancies. On a speculative basis, when comparing nonconvertible preferred stocks with common stocks of the same company, the same tendency for the latter to sell too high can be observed. Comparisons of this kind can be safely drawn, however, only when the preferred stock bears cumulative dividends.

Discrepancies Due to Special Supply and Demand Factors. So far in this chapter, we have been looking at discrepancies in the price caused by traditional changes in supply or demand. Sometimes, however, this can be due to special and temporary factors. As an example, Graham mentions a high-grade railroad issue that became priced relatively differently due to a heavy volume sale of another series.

United States Savings Bonds Offer Similar Opportunity. The disparity between United States Government and corporate obligations has reappeared in recent years. In addition to their safety factor, there are also tax advantages, as well as the opportunity to liquidate in the market at any time, with no intermediate loss in the market, due to the spread.

Chapter 52—Summary

Market Analysis and Security Analysis

In this final chapter of the book, Graham starts by examining whether market analysis can be used as a substitute or an addition to security analysis. Market analysis, which today is also known as "technical analysis," can take two different forms. The first is that past price movement alone can predict the future. Using logical reasoning, Graham discusses this and comes up with four conclusions, culminating in his opinion that it should not be possible.

The second type of market analysis is that other factors outside the market should predict future market prices. Factors that have nothing to do with the stock market are mentioned; i.e., a blast furnace. Clearly there is no causality, and only random correlations can be found. Other indirect factors such as interest rates might have an impact, but here, the problem is the time element. Graham concludes that market analysis is of no use.

Another disadvantage of market analysis as compared to security analysis is that it leaves no margin of safety. In security analysis, the concept will secure that, even if wrong, the investment might still prove satisfactory. In market analysis, the investor loses money immediately if he is wrong. Market analysis also implies that, in order for someone to gain, someone else must lose. It is a repeated game that Graham thinks is based on luck, and therefore one can only be temporarily successful. He concludes by saying that there is no dependable way of making money easily and quickly, either in Wall Street or elsewhere.

Finally in this chapter, Graham provides an overview of investment policies by different classes of investments. Sound investment principles are reintroduced, such as the notion that security analysis consists both of a qualitative and a quantitative analysis, and that the individual investor should not invest in himself if he cannot advise others.

Chapter 52—Outline

Forecasting security prices is not properly a part of security analysis; nevertheless, the two activities are frequently carried out by the same individuals and organizations. Some experts and services confine their aims to predicting longer term in the market; others pay a great deal of attention to the price development of individual issues.

Market Analysis as a Substitute for, or Adjunct to, Security Analysis. If one could foretell the movements of stock prices without reference to values (here called "market analysis"), then it would be more profitable to master this technique than to look at the intrinsic value. One could also argue that in such a situation, security analysis should only be applied for selecting fixed-value investments.

Others believe that the best results can be obtained through market analysis of a stock in conjunction with security analysis of its intrinsic value.

Two Kinds of Market Analysis. The first kind of market analysis makes predictions exclusively from the past actions of the stock market. The second considers all sorts of economic factors; i.e., business conditions, general and specific; money rates; the political outlook.

The underlying theory of the first approach may be summed up in the declaration that "the market is its own best forecaster." In practice, much of this is carried out by reading charts. It must be pointed out that much present-day market analysis represents a combination of the two kinds described, in the sense that the market's action alone constitutes the predominant but not the exclusive field of study. General economic indications play a subordinate but still significant role.

Implication of the First Type of Market Analysis. Market analysis, sometimes called "technical analysis," has increased in popularity. Graham is quite skeptical, and while not saying this explicitly, some of his examples, such as comparing technical analysis with astrology, leave the reader with no doubt as to his opinion.

In this chapter, he looks at the possibility of a study to examine whether past price movements can be used to foretell future movements. Such a study should lead to these conclusions:

1. Chart-reading cannot be a science.

2. It has not proved itself in the past to be a dependable method of making profits in the stock market.

3. Its theoretical basis rests upon faulty logic or else upon mere assertion.

4. Its vogue is due to certain advantages it possesses over haphazard speculation, but these advantages tend to diminish as the number of chart students increases.

1. Chart-reading Is Not a Science and Its Practice Cannot Be Continuously Successful. If it were a science, everybody could predict price changes, and everyone could make money continuously. This is patently impossible. Such predictions would cause human action that would invalidate them.

2. Consequently, it follows that there is no generally known method of chart-reading that has been continuously successful for a long period of time. If this were the case, the method would be speedily adopted by numberless traders. This very following would bring its usefulness to an end.

3. Theoretical Basis Open to Question. The theoretical basis of chart-reading runs:

a. The action of the market (or of a particular stock) reflects the activities and the attitudes of those interested in it.

b. Therefore, by studying records of market action, we can tell what is going to happen next in the market.

This premise may well be true, but the conclusion does not necessarily follow. One can learn technical aspects about stock from charts, but that is not the same as gaining enough information about a security to ensure it will be profitable.

We can compare the examination of a company's past earnings as an indicator for the future to using price movement to predict the future. To some extent they are alike, as they deal with data that are not conclusive to the future. The difference is that the securities analyst can protect himself by a margin of safety that is denied to the market analyst.

4. Other Theoretical and Practical Weaknesses: The plausibility of chart-reading is derived, in Graham's opinion, from gambling, where a typical approach is that losses should be cut short and profits allowed to run. This principle should prevent large losses, and at times enables the making of a large profit. In reality, the gambler will experience that the small losses exceed the large profit over time, simply because the odds are against him.

An additional comment about this approach is that when everyone decides to limit their losses and sell, the market price will rapidly decline, and the average price for those cutting losses would therefore also be lower.

The Second Type of Mechanical Forecasting. The other type of mechanical forecasting is based on factors outside the market. There are also some less plausible theories, such as a blast furnace to predict market prices. Such theories may seem plausible because they have worked in the past; however, since there is no causality, there is no reason to expect that this success should repeat itself.

Another problem occurs when there is causality. It is reasonable to believe that high interest rates will lead to stock market drops. The question is *when will it happen?* There is no scientific answer to that.

Broadly speaking, therefore, the endeavor to forecast security-price changes by reference to mechanical indices is open to the same objections as the methods of the chart readers. They are not truly scientific, because there is no convincing reasoning to support them, and because forecasting in the economic field is a logical impossibility.

Disadvantages of Market Analysis as Compared with Security Analysis: In security analysis, protection is obtained by insisting upon margins of safety, or values well in excess of the price paid. This means that even if the security turns out to be less attractive than it first appeared, it can still be satisfactory. In market analysis there are no margins of safety; you are either right or wrong, and if you are wrong, you lose money.

Another disadvantage is that profits made by trading in the market are for the most part realized at the expense of others who are trying to do the same thing. The market analyst can therefore be hopeful of success only upon the assumption that he will be more clever or perhaps luckier than his competitors.

An advantage for the security analyst is that he examines a far larger list of securities than does the market analyst. Out of this large list, he selects the exceptional cases in which the market price falls far short of reflecting intrinsic value, either through neglect or because of undue emphasis laid upon unfavorable factors that are probably temporary.

An interesting observation is that market analysis seems easier than security analysis, and its rewards may be realized much more quickly. For these very reasons, it is likely to prove more disappointing in the long run. There is no dependable way of making money easily and quickly, either in Wall Street or elsewhere.

Prophesies Based on Near-Term Prospects: A substantial part of analysis advice is given on near-term prospects. The argument is that if the outlook favors increased earnings, the issue should be bought in the expectation that it will increase in price when the actual profit is reported.

The weakness of this argument is that the current market price already takes the consensus of opinion on future prospects into account. And in many cases the prospects would already have driven up the price more than it should.

Graham is skeptical of the ability of the analyst to forecast the market behavior of individual issues over the near-term future. This does not matter if he bases his predictions on the technical position of the market, the general outlook for business, or the specific outlook for the individual companies.

More satisfactory results are to be obtained, in his opinion, by confining the positive conclusions of the security analyst to these fields:

1. The selection of standard senior issues that meet exacting safety tests.
2. The discovery of senior issues that merit an investment rating, but also have opportunities for appreciation in value.

3. The discovery of common stocks or speculative senior issues that appear to be selling at far less than their intrinsic value.

4. The determination of definite price discrepancies between related securities for which situations may justify making exchanges or initiating hedging or arbitrage operations.

A SUMMARY OF OUR VIEWS ON INVESTMENT POLICIES

A. The Investor of Small Means:

1. Investment for Income.

In this case, the only sensible investment, in terms of safety and accumulated income, under present conditions (in 1940), is found in United States Savings Bonds.

Other good investments yield little, if any, more, and they do not have equal protection against both ultimate and intermediate loss.

2. Investment for Profit.

Four approaches are open to both the small and large investor:

a. Purchase of representative common stocks when the market level is clearly low, as judged by objective, long-term standards. This policy requires patience and courage, and is by no means free from the possibility of grave miscalculation.

b. Purchase of individual issues with special growth possibilities, when these can be obtained at reasonable prices in relation to actual accomplishment. The investor must remember that, when growth is generally expected, the price is rarely reasonable.

c. Purchase of well-secured privileged senior issues. A combination of adequate security with a promising conversion or similar right is a rare, but possible. A policy of careful selection in this field should bring good results, provided the investor has the patience and persistence needed to find his opportunities.

d. Purchase of securities selling well below intrinsic value. Intrinsic value takes into account not only past earnings and liquid asset values, but also future earning power, conservatively estimated—in other words, qualitative as well as quantitative elements.

The search for and the recognition of security values of the types just discussed are not beyond the competence of the small investor who wishes to practice security analysis in a non-professional capacity. He will, however, need better-than-average intelligence and training. There is logic in the belief that unless a man is qualified to advise others professionally, he should not prescribe for himself.

3. *Speculation.*

The investor of small means may opt to step out of his role and become a speculator. (He may also opt to regret his actions.) There are various types of speculation, and they offer varying chances of success:

a. Buying stock in new or virtually new ventures. Graham condemns this unhesitatingly and with emphasis. The odds are so strongly against him that he might as well throw three-quarters of the money out of the window and keep the rest in the bank.

b. Trading in the market. It is fortunate for Wall Street as an institution that a small minority of people can trade successfully, but even more fortunate that many others think they can. Graham believes that, regardless of preparation and method, success in trading is accidental and temporary, or else due to a highly uncommon talent. The implication is that the vast majority of stock traders are inevitably doomed to failure. Graham remarks that he does not expect this conclusion to have much effect on the public.

c. Purchase of "growth stocks" at generous prices. The chances of individual success are much brighter here than in the other forms of speculation. That said, as it is considered speculation, this approach is still inherently dangerous.

B. The Individual Investor of Large Means.

Although he has obvious technical advantages over the small investor, he suffers from three specific handicaps:

1. The investor must not only consider United States Savings Bonds, but also the broader field of fixed-value investment. We believe that strict application of quantitative tests, plus reasonably good judgment in the qualitative area should yield a satisfactory end result.

2. Possible inflation is more serious to him than to the small investor. As stocks to some extent are inflation-proof, they can be held as a defensive measure.

3. The size of his investment unit is more likely to induce the large investor to concentrate on popular and active issues.

C. Investment by Business Corporations.

Graham believes that United States Government bonds, which are exempt from corporate income taxes, are almost the only logical medium. It seems fairly evident that other types of investments by business enterprises, be they in bonds or stocks, can offer an appreciably higher return only at the risk of loss and criticism.

D. Institutional Investment.

No policies are suggested here for financial institutions whose business it is to be versed in the theory and practice of investment. Nevertheless, Graham does make the following observation about this difficult issue:

> An institution that can manage to get along on the low income provided by high-grade, fixed-value issues should confine its holdings to this field. It can be doubted if the better performance of common-stock indexes over past periods will, in itself, warrant the heavy responsibilities and the recurring uncertainties that are inseparable from a common-stock investment program.

Themes Found Throughout The Book

- Graham and Dodd (who was initially his "scribe"), emphasize the difference between investing and speculating, and point out that the man of small means cannot afford to lose any of it. Undoubtedly they were influenced by the Wall Street crash, as everyone must have been, but their *caveats* are sound in any financial climate.

***

- The term *analysis* indicates a scientific and methodical study of facts, which results in logical conclusions. But investment is not an exact science, and success derives in part from personal skills and chance.
- Analytical judgments are reached by applying standards to facts.
- The analyst must preserve a sense of proportion, analyze what matters, and ignore what is trivial.
- Separating investing from speculating by definition is not easy; failure to distinguish one from the other has led to tragedies.
- Investments are: bonds; outright purchases; for permanent holding; for income; in safe securities.
- Speculations are: stocks; purchases on margin; for a "quick turn;" for profit; in risky issues.
- Specific standards have to be applied to give meaning to the term "safety."
- An investment operation promises safety of principal and a satisfactory return. Operations not meeting these requirements are speculative.
- An investment operation is one that can be justified on both qualitative and quantitative grounds.
- Investment is founded on the past and present; speculation relies on the future to improve:
- for the investor: the future is to be guarded against rather than profited from;
- for the speculator: he anticipates the future will be better than the past.
- The New York Stock Exchange defines gambling as choosing, without

need, to take a risk (betting on horse racing), whereas speculation is the inherent risk in undertaking an action.

- "Intelligent speculation" is taking a measured risk that seems justified after analysis.
- "Unintelligent speculation" is taking a risk without adequate examination of the situation.
- Safety is measured in terms of the ability of the issuer to meet obligations.
- That ability should be assessed in terms of depression, not prosperity.
- Lack of safety is not compensated by high dividends.
- Avoiding trouble is better than seeking protection after it occurs.
- A sound investment must be able to withstand adversity. Enterprises that have withstood adversity may be favored by investors.
- Investment for Profit: where growth is generally expected, the price is rarely reasonable.
- The investor of small means may opt to step out of his role and become a speculator. He may also opt to regret his actions.

Intrinsic Value Calculation

A large misconception many people have with Security Analysis is they think it contains an intrinsic value formula. As you can see from the summary, no defined calculation or detailed discussion for determining this important value is provided. Although this isn't specifically outlined in the book, I would like to direct your attention to our website, www.BuffettsBooks.com so you can have access to tools that teach investors how to determine the intrinsic value of stocks and bonds. The site is completely free and requires no sign-up to use the tools, so enjoy.

For determining the intrinsic value of common stocks:

1. A discount cash flow model can be found at:

   http://www.buffettsbooks.com/security-analysis/intrinsic-value-calculator-dcf.html

2. A fixed-income calculator adjusted for equities:

   http://www.buffettsbooks.com/intelligent-investor/stocks/intrinsic-value-calculator.html

For determining the intrinsic value of bonds:

http://www.buffettsbooks.com/intelligent-investor/bonds/bond-calculator.html

For determining the intrinsic value of callable preferred stock:

http://www.buffettsbooks.com/intelligent-investor/preferred-shares/value-preferred-stock.html

About The Authors

BENJAMIN GRAHAM

Benjamin Graham was named Benjamin Grossbaum when he was born in London, England to Jewish parents, May 9, 1894. When he was not yet two years old, the family moved to New York City where his father dealt in china dishes and figurines. They prospered, lived on Upper Fifth Avenue, had maidservants—and the young Benjamin even had a French governess. But his father died in 1903, at the age of 35, the business failed and the family home was turned into a boarding house run by his mother, Dorothy, who borrowed money to trade on margin and was wiped out financially—which can only have left a very deep impression on her son about the dangers of the market.

Although they suffered poverty when his father died, Benjamin in 1911, aged 17, won a scholarship to Columbia University, and earned money in part-time jobs as he studied. At the age of 20, he graduated second in his class and was class salutatorian. Despite an offer of a post as an instructor in mathematics and other subjects at Columbia, he entered the finance field, "Wall Street," in 1914 as a runner and board-boy for Newburger, Henderson and Loeb at the New York Stock Exchange. Within a year he was successfully "playing the market," short on this and long on that, and with success.

During World War One it was considered expedient to change the name from the Germanic *Grossbaum* to the Scottish *Graham*.

On Wall Street he was initially a clerk in a bond-trading firm, then became an analyst, a partner, and eventually started the Graham-Newman Partnership, an open-end mutual fund that was later closed to new investors. Within 15 years, he became wealthy, and with his partner, Newman, controlled five million dollars in capital and hedged positions.

Although he had his triumphs in personal investing, he suffered, as did many others, in the "Great Crash" of 1929-32, and sustained 70% losses. His corporation, the Graham-Newman Partnership, had one of the best long-term records in history, and reported annual earnings of 14.7% compared with 12.2% for the market.

He taught at Columbia University's Graduate School of Business from 1928 through to 1957; there he popularized the need to examine price-to-earnings (P/E) ratios, debt-to-equity ratios, dividend records, book values, and earnings growth.

Graham is considered the first proponent of value investing, an investment approach he began teaching at Columbia Business School in 1928 and subsequently refined with David Dodd. *Security Analysis*, with David Dodd, and *The Intelligent Investor*, published in 1949, are his two most widely acclaimed books.

Graham's favorite allegory is that of Mr. Market, a fellow who turns up every day at the stockholder's door offering to buy or sell his shares at a different price. Usually, the price quoted by Mr. Market seems plausible, but occasionally it is ridiculous. The investor is free to either agree with his quoted price and trade with him, or to ignore him completely. Mr. Market doesn't mind this, and will be back the following day to quote another price. The point is that the investor should not regard the whims of Mr. Market as determining the value of the shares that the investor owns. He should profit from market folly rather than participate in it. The investor is best off concentrating on the real-life performance of his companies and receiving dividends, rather than being too concerned with Mr. Market's often irrational behavior.

In recent years, Graham's "Mr. Market" approach has been challenged by Modern Portfolio Theory (MPT), based on the hypothesis of efficiency of financial markets, which is widely taught in American and British business schools, and posits that it is generally impossible for any individual to consistently outwit the market, thus denying the possibility of any distinction between "market price" and "value" of a security.

Warren Buffett, who credits Graham as grounding him with a sound intellectual investment framework, described him as the second most influential person in his life after his own father, and wrote, "A remarkable aspect of Ben's dominance of his professional field was that he achieved it without that narrowness of mental activity that concentrates all effort on a single end. It was, rather, the incidental by-product of an intellect whose breadth almost exceeded definition. Certainly I have never met anyone with a mind of similar scope. Virtually total recall, unending fascination with new knowledge, and an ability to recast it in a form applicable to seemingly unrelated problems made exposure to his thinking in any field a delight."

According to Warren Buffett, Graham said that he wished every day to do something foolish, something creative, and something generous. Buffett said that Graham excelled most at the last.

He died September 21, 1976, in Aix-en-Provence, France.

Graham is the author of:

> *Security Analysis*, editions 1934, 1940, 1951, 1962, 1988, 2008
>
> *The Intelligent Investor*, editions 1949, reprinted in 2005; 1959, 1965, 1973

Storage and Stability: A Modern Ever-Normal Granary, New York: McGraw Hill. 1937

The Interpretation of Financial Statements

World Commodities and World Currency, 1944

Benjamin Graham, the Memoirs of the Dean of Wall Street

DAVID LEFEVRE DODD

The less well-known co-author of *Security Analysis,* David Dodd was born August 23, 1895 in Berkeley County, West Virginia. He was a student in the high school at Martinsburg, where his father was the principal. After graduation in 1916, he was in the US Navy during the First World War from 1917 to 1919, and was a commissioned officer after serving as a seaman.

In 1920, he completed his Bachelor of Science, at University of Pennsylvania, and from 1921 to 1922, he was research assistant for an economist at the National Bank of Commerce in New York. He continued his studies and in 1922 he received his Master of Science at Columbia University where he continued as a student and teacher:

> 1922 to 1925: junior faculty position as Instructor in Economics
>
> 1925 to 1930: Instructor in Finance
>
> 1926 to 1945: in charge of the business and economics courses
>
> 1930: received his PhD; Benjamin Graham was his academic advisor
>
> 1930 to 1938: Assistant Professor of Finance
>
> 1938 to 1947: Associate Professor
>
> 1947 to 1961: Professor
>
> 1948 to 1952: Associate Dean, Columbia Business School
>
> 1961: retired as Professor Emeritus, Finance
>
> 1984: Doctor of Letters (hon.caus.)

David Dodd was also active in private financial affairs from as early as 1928 when he was advising private clients, and then between the years 1950 -1959 was in partnership with his co-author Benjamin Graham.

David Dodd was in Portland, Maine when he died on September 1988 at the age of 93.

About The Book

The Wall Street Crash of 1929 (Black Thursday) almost wiped out Graham, who had started teaching the year before at his alma mater, Columbia. The crash inspired Graham to search for a more conservative, safer way to invest—something he had already advocated in articles written for financial journals. Graham agreed to teach at Columbia with the stipulation that someone take notes. Dodd, then a young instructor at Columbia, volunteered, and later completed his PhD under Graham's guidance. Those transcriptions served as the basis for the book *Security Analysis*, which promoted the concept of value investing, and which, despite the changes brought about by three-quarters of a century, remains in print and in use as a teaching guide today. As such, it is the longest-running investment text ever published.

Publication history by McGraw Hill

1934: 1ˢᵗ ed. Whittlesey House (the trade division of McGraw-Hill)

> Black bound cover (1st printing) by The Maple Press Co., York, PA, for a small distribution in the United States

> Maroon bound cover (2nd printing) was published for sale abroad, The Maple Press Co.

> Reprint editions 1996 & 1997

1940: 2ⁿᵈ ed.; Reprint 2002

1951: 3ʳᵈ ed.; Reprint 1976 & 2004

1962: 4ᵗʰ ed. (Charles Sidney Cottle, co-author)

1988: 5ᵗʰ ed. (updated by Cottle, Murray, and Block)

2008: 6ᵗʰ ed. (commentary by 10 contributors)

According to James Grant in the 6ᵗʰ edition, not until five months after publication of the *Security Analyst* did it receive a review in the *New York Times,* which, although enthusiastic about the book, was "rueful" about the general state of post-crash finances.

THE SUMMARY AUTHORS

linkedin.com/in/prestonpysh

Preston Pysh is a financial investing author and the co-host of *TheInvestorsPodcast.com*. He has published multiple international best selling books and is the founder of the Pylon Holding Company. He runs the free educational website, BuffettsBooks.com, which teaches students how to invest in stocks and bonds like the billionaire Warren Buffett.

Author of

Warren Buffett's Three Favorite Books

Warren Buffett Accounting Book

A Summary of the Intelligent Investor

A Summary of Security Analysis

The Diary of a West Point Cadet

linkedin.com/in/stigbrodersen

Stig Brodersen holds a master's degree in Finance and has studied Business Analysis at Harvard University. Stig is a co-host of *TheInvestorsPodcast.com* and works as a college professor teaching financial accounting, investments, and economics. Stig is the founder of the Stig Brodersen Holding Company and BuffettsBooks.com.

Author of

Warren Buffett Accounting Book

A Summary of the Intelligent Investor

A Summary of Security Analysis

RECOMMENDED READINGS

One Up On Wall Street – by Peter Lynch

The Neatest Little Guide to Stock Market Investing – by Jason Kelly

The Intelligent Investor – by Benjamin Graham

Common Stocks and Uncommon Profits – by Phillip Fisher

Buffett: The Making of an American Capitalist – by Roger Lowenstein

The Snowball – By Alice Schroeder

Berkshire Hathaway Letters to Shareholders – by Warren Buffett

CPSIA information can be obtained
at www.ICGtesting.com
Printed in the USA
BVHW040538240620
582140BV00007B/485